Always, Brenda

Handbags

Handbags

WHAT EVERY WOMAN SHOULD KNOW

STEPHANIE PEDERSEN

D&C

David and Charles

A DAVID & CHARLES BOOK

David & Charles is an F+W Publications Inc.
company
4700 East Galbraith Road
Cincinnati, OH 45236

First published in the UK in 2006
Copyright © Studio Cactus 2006

Stephanie Pedersen has asserted her right to be
identified as author of this work in accordance
with the Copyright, Designs and Patents Act,
1988.

A catalogue record for this book is available
from the British Library.

ISBN-13: 978-0-7153-295-0 hardback
ISBN-10: 0-7153-2495-0 hardback

Printed in Singapore by Star Standard
for David & Charles
Brunel House   Newton Abbot   Devon

Visit our website at
www.davidandcharles.co.uk

David & Charles books are available from all
good bookshops; alternatively you can contact
our Orderline on 0870 9908222 or write to us at
FREEPOST EX2 110, D & C Direct, Newton
Abbot, TQ12 4ZZ (no stamp required UK only);
US customers call 800-289-0963 and Canadian
customers call 800-840-5220.

Contents

Elegance and Intrigue

If you're a bag lover, you know that the quickest, most gorgeous way to add panache to your look is with the right handbag. Modern handbags are as much about function as they are about self-expression and even status. A burnished brown Birkin? A home-sewn tote with purple appliqués? A vintage clutch? A great bag in every colour for perfect wardrobe coordination? Today, anything goes!

Introduction

The handbag: a brief history

What started out as a way for early men and women to carry food, tools and money slowly evolved into an accessory that can make or break an outfit. To the modern girl about town, handbags are now more about style than their original functional role as practical receptacles.

Purses, handbags, totes, bags, pocketbooks – whatever you call them, these utilitarian sacs have been around as long as humans have. Early models were made of animal skin, crude fabric, or even tree bark fashioned into a kind of pouch.

Options appear

As people's lives became more intricate, so too did their bags. Blacksmiths began carrying sturdy carry-alls, nuns and monks small alms bags, and high-bred ladies, gorgeously decorated purses. Drawstring pouches of all kinds were popular (and still are!), and while some people (especially men who worked outdoors) carried practical leather bags, textile sacs were the style of choice.

CLOTH DRAWSTRING POUCH
Soft sacs like these have been used since the beginning of time. They're so versatile that we continue to use drawstring bags even today.

HANDBAGS OF THE 20TH CENTURY

1900s
This swingy reticule is a soft fabric purse suspended by a long wrist chain.

1910s
Another reticule, this velvet bag features a metal frame and clasp closure.

1920s
Flappers needed purses that would stay on a hand or wrist while dancing the charleston.

1930s
Fabric bags, such as this slim black crepe number with diamanté clasp, were especially trendy.

1940s
Wartime rationing meant 'make do and mend'. This cheery bag is fashioned from dyed raffia.

1950s
Extreme femininity took over fashion. Purses become rigid with short handstraps.

The modern handbag

Throughout the centuries, women have carried small soft bags decorated with needlepoint and embroidery. At first these were hand-held. Some, called pockets, were tucked into openings in a skirt. Towards the 18th century, however, clothing took on a slimmer silhouette. Ladies could no longer hide bags in their dresses. Soon, everyone carried a handbag. (Every female, that is. The appearance of trouser pockets meant that men no longer needed bags.) Handbags were further changed by fashion trends. Different eras favoured different materials. Fabric and natural fibres during the war years, plastics in the 1950s and 1960s, leather in the late 20th and early 21st centuries. Clutches were must-haves in the 1940s and 1980s, slim boxes were *en mode* in the 1930s and 1950s, whimsical bags showed up in the 1960s and 1990s. The obsessive, lust for designer bags? Well, that distinction belongs firmly to the 21st century.

> " . . . maybe the best any of us can do is not quit, play the hand we've been dealt, and accessorize what we've got. "

CARRIE BRADSHAW, SEX AND THE CITY

1960s
Mod-style and flower-power led to all kinds of choices including this trippy look by Pucci.

1970s
The earthy 1970s feature a DIY aesthetic. Simple handmade and homespun bags are in.

1980s
Power dressing brings strong looks. Clutch and no-fuss briefcase purses are *de rigeur*.

1990s
Quirky purses celebrate the expressiveness of the 1990s, encompassing everything from grunge to glam.

2000s
Bling, bling and more bling. High-status labels, showy design flourishes and look-at-me colours like spangly metallics and white are in demand.

What your bag says about you

The bag you carry tells people who you are – for better or worse! Show yourself off to your best advantage: The next time you step out, give extra thought to what your bag is saying about you.

THE DESIGNER BAG
You know what's hot before *Vogue*! Avoid fashion burn-out by occasionally going for the cloth purse your auntie made.

How important is 'the right bag'? What could 'the right bag' possibly mean? One thing's for certain, a good bag is lovingly tended, well made and looks fabulous. It doesn't have to match whatever else you're wearing, but it must at least complement your getup. Yes, this does matter. Put another way: How many times have you purchased a purse without regard to the rest of your wardrobe? Handbags are supposed to be accessories, a condiment to add panache to the main course. In other words, the bag must work with the outfit. Take time to choose your bag.

THE BACKPACK
Warm, casual and busy, you are young in years – or at heart. A backpack (even if it's Prada) will never work with a gown, but a designer version adds flare to office trousers or a denim skirt.

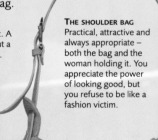

THE SHOULDER BAG
Practical, attractive and always appropriate – both the bag and the woman holding it. You appreciate the power of looking good, but you refuse to be like a fashion victim.

" *She had the loaded handbag of someone who camps out and seldom goes home, or who imagines life must be full of emergencies* "

MAVIS GALLAENT, CANADIAN AUTHOR

THE COLOURFUL TOTE

You're fun, youthful, and generous, with things to do, places to go. If you'd like a more chic persona, try a well-made leather tote in a neutral shade.

THE BUMBAG

A bumbag says frumpy. It says tourist. Some advice: A long-strapped bag worn across the body provides the security you crave without making you a fashion 'don't'.

THE CLUTCH

You are confident, a man's woman who just may allow him to hold your keys, lighter, and whatever else won't fit into your showy bag.

CROCHETED BAG

You're easy-going with an arty, nurturing bent. People love you, animals love you. If you're feeling taken advantage of, carry a clutch. It could give you perspective.

ETHNIC STYLE
You are strong in both will and personality, you know what you want and how to get it. If you feel people are avoiding you, carry a tote.

It can be difficult to always style your bag with your outfit, especially when some of today's hottest handbags cost more than the total of every single article of clothing we own!

Advice for handbag addicts

Do you have more handbags than shirts? More purses than pants? Consider reversing the formula: Buy your handbags first, then plan your outfits around them. Yes, it goes against the advice of fashion

THE STATEMENT PURSE
You have a natural sense of proportion and fashion; people look to you for clothing tips. Consider charging for your advice!

"I'm homeless! I'll be a bag lady! A Fendi bag lady, but a bag lady!!"

CARRIE BRADSHAW, SEX AND THE CITY

OBJET D'ART
Metallic bags are showy. When done up in an unusual shape with an unusual handle, they are even showier. Be careful that you aren't letting your bag do all your fashion work for you.

Building a bag wardrobe

Do you need more than one handbag? Choose a neutral, reasonably sized shoulder bag and one is all you'll need. But most of us want more than that. In fact, the average woman now owns four to six handbags. Consider:

• One evening bag. Be on the lookout for something metallic, sparkly or black. Clutches are great for night-time.

• A work bag. Look at what your boss is toting and find something similar. Only be creative if it suits your job.

• Something fun for weekends and play days. Maybe a brightly coloured hobo, a souvenir tote, a backpack.

• A gym bag or baby changing bag that is polished enough to look smart at all times and fun to carry.

SHOPPING WITH A FRIEND
Shopping with a pal can be great fun. However, it's best to go with someone whose opinion you trust, whose fashion-sense you appreciate and who is smart about money.

'experts' everywhere, but give it a try. If you choose your handbag wisely, you can afford to buy one good purse that you really love but that also updates your look. At least you'll have put some thought into your wardrobe. Not a bad thing at all – and a damned good way to make sure that your bags and clothing complement each other. At least slightly!

Have fun

All this said, fashion isn't neurobiology. It's simply a fun way to express yourself. You might fancy a style change and a new bag can do that for you. You want to carry a découpage poodle with a handle to work? Do it. You want to pair a studded hobo bag with an evening gown? Go right ahead. Your life. Your style. Handbags are meant to help with both. And there's certainly nothing wrong with going your own way now and again instead of always following those fashion pages to the letter.

STRAW BASKET
Natural, maternal, and sensitive, you are the go-to girl for all your friends.

SPORTS BAG
You are athletic – at least in mind. If you feel unnoticed, borrow your sister's clutch.

Handbags of Yore

For as long as we've needed to carry things, handbags have existed. Practical sacs, to carry food and other necessities, were worn by men and women alike. As time passed, bag designs became ever more glamorous – from sheepskin purses to charm-laden chatelaines. With the invention of interior trouser pockets in the late 1700s, handbags became the sole preserve of women. Men's loss!

1 *Pre-1900*

Pouches and purses

There are no breath mints, car keys haven't been invented, credit cards don't exist, and no one knows what lip gloss, mobile phones, Blackberries or iPods are. Bags don't need to be big!

That's not to say, however, that bags weren't important during the medieval era. Clothing pockets hadn't been thought up, so men and women carried small pouches into which they tucked daily necessities such as a handkerchief,

FRAMED POUCH
Some early bags had an iron or silver frame for a more structured look. A belt pin and chain attached the bag to a belt.

paternoster (rosary beads), maybe a prayer book or a wax tablet for writing, or even a knife. And not forgetting money. Hence the name *aumônières*, almoners purses, or alms purses. The term originated in Europe during the 13th and 14th centuries, when the poor and needy begged openly on city streets. The most fashionable purses of the period were made of elaborately embroidered textiles – often boasting gold thread, sometimes carrying pious mottoes. The rich carrying these bags would stop and give money – alms – to the needy.

SARACEN ALMS PURSE
'Saracen' here refers to the elaborate silk and gold embroidery, which many think originated in Arab countries and came to Europe through trade with Moorish countries.

Drawstring bags

Square-shaped drawstring bags were the among the most popular medieval bag designs, beloved by both men and women. Sometimes carried by hand, they were more often tied around a belt or waist sash, or attached by means of a metal belt frame. Other period faves included the medieval bum bag, known as a shepherd's budget: 'shepherd' because shepherds carried in them their knives and necessities – even shorn wool – and 'budget' from the French word *bougette*, meaning a sack. These were much better-looking than today's nylon zippered bum bags. Really!

GAMING PURSES
Drawstring satchels, like these rounded pouches, were popular for carrying coins. Made of cloth or sometimes leather, they were typically knotted around a belt. Some historians call them gaming purses. Others suspect that this design might be that referred to by the Anglo term 'hamondey', which was used briefly during the 14th century.

Function and frivolity

From scissors to sewing needles to kitchen tools, the hausfraus, young lovelies, and crones of the late Renaissance have much to carry.

But pockets hadn't been invented. And neither had deodorant, nor the concept of regular bathing. But not to worry – women (even those centuries older than us) are nothing if not resourceful. To counteract pungent

SILK EMBROIDERED PURSE
Gorgeous, simply structured bags, like this dating from around 1600, were fashioned at home and decorated by the owner with fine needlework.

'THE CHATELAINE; A REALLY USEFUL PRESENT' (*PUNCH* 1849)
The *chatelaine* was a web of chains that held a variety of implements.

body odour, females of the late 16th to 17th centuries carried elaborately embroidered sweet bags. These small pouches were stuffed with fragrant potpourri and were usually tied around a waist sash. Similar embroidered bags, often squarer in shape and larger in size, were also kept handy. Known as workbags, they carried a lady's 'fancy work' and mending. Ladies of yesteryear liked to keep busy!

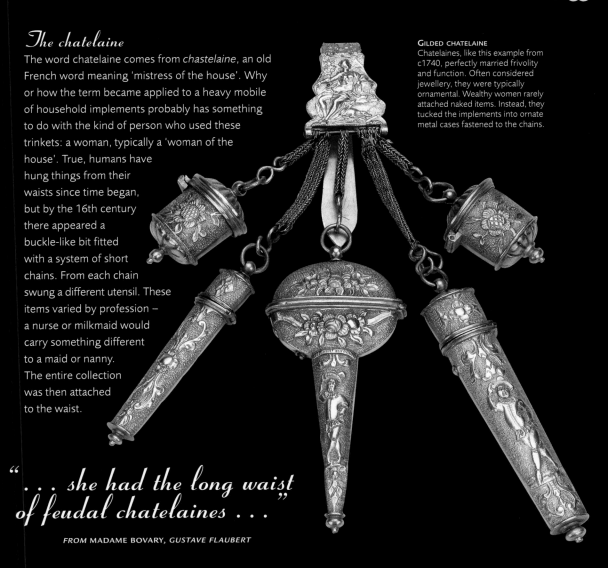

The chatelaine

The word chatelaine comes from *chastelaine*, an old French word meaning 'mistress of the house'. Why or how the term became applied to a heavy mobile of household implements probably has something to do with the kind of person who used these trinkets: a woman, typically a 'woman of the house'. True, humans have hung things from their waists since time began, but by the 16th century there appeared a buckle-like bit fitted with a system of short chains. From each chain swung a different utensil. These items varied by profession – a nurse or milkmaid would carry something different to a maid or nanny. The entire collection was then attached to the waist.

GILDED CHATELAINE

Chatelaines, like this example from c1740, perfectly married frivolity and function. Often considered jewellery, they were typically ornamental. Wealthy women rarely attached naked items. Instead, they tucked the implements into ornate metal cases fastened to the chains.

" *. . . she had the long waist of feudal chatelaines . . .* "

FROM MADAME BOVARY, *GUSTAVE FLAUBERT*

Bags beneath clothes

The neoclassical period is alive with possibility. Romance is on every artist's and thinker's mind, and gentility is the ideal of the day. At least it is among the comfortable classes, who can enjoy such refinements.

The 17th and 18th centuries were a time of good living for the genteel classes. Men and women spent their considerable spare time debating lofty concepts such as romantic love, beauty, manners and morals. People had time to play, be it the harpsichord, a game of cards, or a monthly ball. Clothing mirrored the tenor of the times by growing prissier. Skirts got bigger and more voluminous, bodices got tighter, sleeves fussier. No longer did women loop pouches into the band of a dress. Oh no, an obvious lump of a bag at the waist would throw off an outfit's proportions. Instead, fashionable ladies favoured more discreet purses called pockets, which they tucked into slits in the folds of their gowns. Though hidden, these bags were ornate, with hand embroidery. As the 18th century approached, beading became another popular bag decoration.

LINEN TIE POCKET
So pretty, so dainty, so feminine. This pocket is embroidered with silk and was made in England between 1725 and 1750.

Oh, the reticule!

When dresses began to slim down towards the end of the 18th century, there weren't billows enough to hold pocket purses. Enter the reticule or *sabretache*. A reticule could be round or square, tasselled or plain, woven, crocheted, or knitted. They were typically decorated with spangles, beads, or embroidery. Some had handles and were carried by hand, others had hooks to attach to a waistband.

ORNATE VELVET BAG
This exquisite bag with a silver frame and hook dating from c1773 is indicative of the examples popular at the end of the 18th century, when dresses became slimmer. It would be just as at home in a modern woman's wardrobe.

LEATHER AND SILK LETTERCASE
You never know when a good line of poetry might come in handy! This romantic leather and silk lettercase, made in France in 1806, features embroidery, a poem and a miniature.

Neoclassical elegance

Pompeii, rediscovered in 1748, is excavated and reconstructed throughout the 19th century. Everyone wants to be an ancient Greek or Roman – or at least look like one.

Ah, the classics! Europeans and Americans of the late 18th and 19th century were obsessed with the ancient Greeks and Romans. The younger generations copied the elders' painting styles, they constructed their buildings with old-style columns, they wrote books mimicking the methods of Plato, Aristotle and Socrates. And clothing – especially that worn by women – morphed into something soft, diaphanous and columnar in a nod to the garb of antiquity.

THE GREEK DRESS
This neoclassical gown provides the perfect slim look but is no good for hanging a purse beneath. Not to worry – ladies adapted by carrying their reticules.

SILK WORKING BAG WITH NEEDLEWORK TOOLS
This pretty bag from c1830, with its hand embroidery and jaunty tassels, was typical of the dainty utility bags carried by young ladies of good breeding.

NEOCLASSICAL LADY
Sliding a bag under this dress from the early 1800s would leave people wondering about that lump. It's a shame no one thought of head-purses – a bag could've been easily tucked into the hat!

There wasn't much room in these body-skimming fashions to stash a pocket-purse. Nor did the gowns' under-the-breast empire waists allow a lady to hang her bag from her sash. Instead, women began carrying their bags by hand. The handbag as we know it was born!

The most popular of these hand-carried bags was the utility or working bag, in which women stashed supplies, including needles, thread, embroidery, mending and letters. These utility bags were typically made from silk, gauze, muslin or cotton, and covered with embroidery. Most featured a drawstring closure, though some had metal clasps. Designs varied widely, with some featuring tassels, loop handles or even beading.

Females of the period had ways to look busy. Whenever in company, they'd reach into their utility bags for something to do. Many ladies, having already finished every last stitch, sat intently knotting, unknotting and reknotting embroidery thread.

GUILD OF BAGS
In nearly every European country there were guilds dedicated to purse making and decorating. Not hard to believe when you study the ornateness of this beauty.

Elaborate design

Early reticules were plain and featured simple closures. Indeed, the word itself comes from the Latin *reticulum*, which means 'small string bag'. In the days of ancient Greece and Rome, the reticulum was as modest as it sounded: a mesh tote to carry provisions. But in time, the bag became smaller and more ornate. Many historians cite the mid-18th century as when the modern reticule first appeared in its more exciting incarnation. The mesh was traded for silk and the string replaced with a cord or chain. Women carried bags just like these right up until the 20th century.

The nineteenth century

The 1800s feature the dainty sensibilities of the Victorian era. Then, as time rolls towards the end of the century, the rough and tumble of the Industrial Revolution starts to have an impact.

The most popular bags of the early 1800s were reticule-style, festooned with beads or embroidery. These dangled from strings or dainty chains and featured a drawstring or metal clasp closure. But there was another flashy option: mesh bags in the style of miser's purses were also popular among early 19th century females. These bags didn't hold much. Then again, they didn't need to: women of the day didn't do much out of doors, nor did they venture far without servants or parents or a big brother or two, any of whom could haul around whatever a proper lass needed.

LONG PURSE OF WHITE GLASS BEADS
This feminine version of the miser's purse hails from France, around the early 19th century. It features tassels of decorative gold-coloured metal beads, as well as gilt ring closures.

A change of pace

With the appearance of steam trains, passenger ships and paddle boats, the late 19th century was all about movement. Women-on-the-go needed bags and carry-alls to contain their possessions. Hatboxes were wildly popular. Belt bags, modelled on the intricate chatelaines of the previous century, were a boon for travellers who needed to keep money, receipts and other necessities safe and easily accessible. Trunks started to show up everywhere. Among the period's most-loved examples were large wicker-woven trunks known affectionately as hand trunks or rail baskets. Wood was another favourite material,

THE RAILWAY BELLE
A helpful porter carries this lady's hand trunk, while her large rail basket sits waiting. No word on who helped Ms Belle get that skirt through the train's doors!

along with leather. Some rail baskets were restrainedly plain, others were decorated with beads, embroidery, painting, embossing, or various types of handles, including gold, coloured leather, or woven straps.

The baby in the basket

In its early years, there was much debate about the health effects of rail travel. Opponents claimed it was harried, violent and stressful. In 1894 Oscar Wilde wrote *The Importance of Being Earnest*, which critics claim is probably his greatest work. The premise? What happens when a flustered female leaves a baby in a bag at London's busy Victoria Station.

EMBOSSED LEATHER BELT WITH TWO BAGS
This hails from Germany in the 1890s. Ladies-on-the-go needed an easy way to carry their money and other small valuables safely.

WOVEN RAIL BASKETS
From France come these two late 19th-century rail baskets both made from straw, wood and leather. The smaller features golden beads and a gold-finished handle.

La Belle Époque

'The beautiful era': it was a pretty time indeed, everything so attractive – and that includes the handbags. There were etched metal clutches, intricate mesh offerings, more beaded and embroidered numbers, a brief infatuation with fur and the invention of gorgeous travel bags, many by designers that are still going strong today. Ever heard of Louis Vuitton?

2 *1900–1919*

Full steam ahead

1901

The Victorian era comes to an end. The moneyed set continues the pursuit of leisure and the demand for luxury luggage starts to grow. Consumerism has begun.

It was the dawn of the 20th century and luxury was the word. Yes, there were 'have-nots', but it was the 'haves' who were driving trends. Among these trends was a penchant for entertainment. The most convenient amusements of the day were trips to the theatre and the opera. Special opera cases were snapped up by those who could afford a bag made for the opera. (Everyone else took their regular handbags.) These cases held opera glasses, a fan and maybe paper and a pencil.

OFF TO THE OPERA
This handy opera case is another offshoot of a luxury life. A special case just to take to the opera? *Mais oui!* But a regular evening bag worked just as well.

SWEDISH LLOYD LINE
ROYAL MAIL AND PASSENGER ROUTE
TO
GOTHENBURG

PASSENGER SHIPS
Ocean liners reached new heights of opulence. The most popular routes tended to be between England and the Eastern United States, but there were many others including this one to Sweden.

Anchors away

Whether it was a boat trip down the Seine, a Continental tour or passage on a transatlantic liner, travel was the preferred leisure of the middle- and upper-incomed classes. However, the clothing of the day was big, layered and hard to pack and trunks for travelling were cumbersome and heavy.

All bags on board

Enter Louis Vuitton, who did his apprenticeship with a Parisian trunk maker before getting a job as 'special clothes packer' to the French Empress Eugenie, wife of Emperor Napoleon III. Frustrated with the day's awkward luggage, he created flat, stackable steamer trunks (some of which were complete with drawers and fold-out desks!) that could be stowed securely in a ship's

"It's in the bag"

LOUIS VUITTON, WHEN ASKED WHAT MADE HIS LUGGAGE SO POPULAR

LOUIS VUITTON ADVERTISING
This is a magazine advert for one of Louis Vuitton's first successes – the canvas steamer bag.

THE FIRST STEAMER BAG
Louis Vuitton's design was originally made as a laundry bag of sorts, meant to tuck into a steamer trunk or hang on the back of a steamship cabin door where it would then be filled with dirty clothes.

hold. The Empress loved his trunks, her friends loved them, and the brand took off as the luggage of choice for the wealthy. Today, Louis Vuitton luggage remains as popular as ever. Many of the original styles are still available and the vintage versions have become highly collectable.

THE FAMOUS 'LV' MONOGRAM
Monogrammed canvas, shown here fashioned into a suitcase with leather trim, was created by Louis Vuitton's son George in an attempt to outsmart counterfeiters. Yes, fake Vuitton bags existed even in those days!

Make mine mesh

1912

The first skyscraper, cross-channel air crossing and North Pole conquest all occur. This year also sees the arrival of the first automatic mesh maker. Bag lovers rejoice!

Mesh is an ancient material, used at least since knights wore it in the Middle Ages. Their contemporaries had practical mesh bags, as well, and the material never went out of fashion. By 1908, women were still carrying them, just as their grandmothers had in the 1700s.

Innovations in mesh

Before 1912, mesh-making was an intricate hand process. Skinny strips of iron, silver, bronze, gold, gunmetal or other metal would be hammered flat then fashioned into interlocking rings. At this rate, it took at least a week to make enough mesh to design the simplest of purses. No wonder they were expensive!

Enter Whiting & Davis, which began in 1879 as a maker of mesh jewellery before gaining acclaim for its chain-mail bags. In 1912, the company developed an automatic mesh-making machine, placing chain-mail bags firmly within reach of middle- and lower-income ladies. Aggressive marketers, Whiting & Davis further fuelled desire with witty advertising slogans. The company is still in business today, weaving mesh mostly for industrial and medical concerns.

MESH: ALWAYS IN STYLE

VICTORIAN SILVER PLATE MESH
This Arts and Crafts roses evening bag was made around 1875. With its ornate frame and soft silhouette, this square bag could dress up even the simplest of gowns.

STERLING SILVER CHAIN MAIL
This soft purse-pouch bag features pleats, which were very hard to achieve with mesh. It also has a chain handle, and a clasp closure.

"The loveliest of all feminine accessories — the perfect mesh!"

WHITING & DAVIS ADVERTISING SLOGAN

AN EVENING OUT – IN WHITING & DAVIS STYLE
This Arts and Crafts mesh and enamel bag, circa 1900, is ideal for opera glasses. The pocket-style oblong bag was fancy and practical.

DIAMANTES ARE A GIRL'S BEST FRIEND
Ah, the diamante clasp. A *de rigeur* way to dress up a bag's closure in the 1930s. This Whiting & Davis evening bag from 1934 is a seriously pretty purse, eh?

Handbags and hobble skirts

1910

Orville and Wilbur Wright's aeroplane has really taken off. Tight Geisha gowns of the Orient are in vogue. Together, these inspire a new, uncomfortable kind of glamour.

In 1910, French clothing designer Paul Poiret created a new way to torture women – the hobble skirt. The inspiration for this floor-length pencil skirt came from two unrelated places. The first was early female aviators, such as Mrs Hart Berg and Wright sister Katherine, who used rope to bind the bottom of their voluminous skirts so the cloth wouldn't flap freely and interfere with flying. The second was the cheongsams and Geisha gowns of Asia, a region that fascinated Poiret.

Hobbling by day

Did anyone wear hobble skirts? Yes – society women, artists, fashionistas and others who wanted to stay *au courant*. A medium to large tapestry or leather bag, often with a cord handle. completed the look.

JAPANESE DELICACY
This grey suede bag from c1910 shows a hand-painted Japanese landscape. It has a handle to wear over the wrist and a silver closure.

A FRUITY LITTLE NUMBER!
This is an Art Nouveau celluloid, fruit-shaped evening bag. Its silk body and handle make it fragile – but so gorgeous!

Hobbling by night

Evening garb was typically sewn from high-sheen fabric and paired with a jacket or shawl. The bag was dainty: usually a small, reticule-style purse with a cord. Shaped as pouches, fruits or other small objects, these were cloth or mesh and hand decorated.

SLAVES OF FASHION.

Ethel. "Lend me your hanky, Mabel." *Mabel.* "Haven't you one in your bag?"
Ethel. "Good gracious, my dear girl, do you think I should put anything in this bag? It's as much as I can carry empty!"

IT'S NO JOKE!
In this *Punch* cartoon, corset-wearing women weighed down by ridiculously large hats and almost overbalanced by their heavy bags are forced to mince about by their hobble skirts.

CLOTH EVENING BAG
A very interesting feature of this bag from c1908 is its gilt metal gate frame with metal flip-up clasp. This opens into a square shape. It's nice to be different.

HAND-EMBROIDERED PETITE POINT BAG
This pretty bag features velvet edging, a jewelled frame and an unexpected lavender interior.

EDWARDIAN TAPESTRY POCHETTE HANDBAG
This 1908 bag has metallic braid edging, a metallic cloth-covered button fastening and a silk lining. It was designed to be worn from the wrist.

If it walks, wear it

1918

World War I comes to an end. In response to wartime austerity, fashion starts to go wild with a trend for using skins, feathers and fur to create everything from bags to hats.

Feathers, reptile skins and fur were very popular – especially as trimmings – during the early years of the 20th century. But these animal offerings were strictly upmarket, worn only by the wealthy. World War I changed all this. As women were forced to become more independent, the petite cloth reticule-style bags of the genteel, feminine Gibson Girl were useless. Women needed room for their things! But due to rationing, leather was in short supply, so designers turned their attention to other animals. When it came to handbags, reptiles were the natural choice. They

HEADS UP
An alligator clutch from the 1920s shows off the versatility of reptile skin. The fashion for attaching the animal's head to a bag seems rather gruesome today but was considered stylish at the time.

were readily available, and few people had much sympathy for the cold-blooded beasts. Soon the skins of snakes, crocodiles, alligators, lizards – even non-reptiles like sharks, fish and armadillos – were being killed to create gorgeous bags. As women became more comfortable carrying skins, designers even used animals' heads.

Faking it

The relentless pursuit of animal hides has, sadly, led to the some species becoming endangered or even extinct. Today we understand the importance of conservation and, fortunately for the fashion industry, there are amazing alternative fake hides.

MAKE IT SNAPPY
This alligator bag, circa 1930, illustrates the lasting popularity of reptile skin. As for the head? A sure-fire way to deter pick-pocketing.

COVER FROM *VOGUE*, **AUGUST 1917**
As this graphic illustration shows, fur was as popular with the *Vogue* editor of the time as it is with the magazine's editor today. Unfortunately, fashion continues to embrace fur.

FOXY LADY!
Why bother with the jacket when you can drape one or more deceased foxes or other small mammals around your shoulders and call it a wrap?

CANADIAN FUR COMPANY ADVERT FROM 1918
A big fur year, what with all the people looking for something luxurious and warm with which to celebrate the end of WWI.

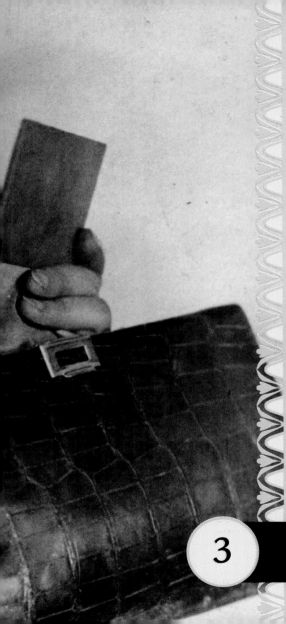

The Jazz Age

Ah, gilded youth. Fun, frivolity and a high regard for shock value pushed their way into the social conscience, leaving behind the stifled, boring mores of the *belle époque* and Victorian eras. Suddenly, women ditched their heavy bags for small, swingy numbers. Purses that they could dance with. Purses just large enough to hold a tawdry tube of lipstick, a mirrored compact and a few cigarettes. Society, and handbags, would never be the same again.

3 *1920–1939*

Night and day

1923

Nightlife comes alive thanks to a generation bent on drinking and dancing the night away. Illegal alcohol, cheeky females and the Charleston are hallmarks of the era.

The flappers created a new, freer femininity. They did things women previously didn't – or couldn't – do. They smoked, drank, spoke when they wanted to and went out unchaperoned. Even at night! They cut their hair boyishly short, wore make-up, eschewed traditional female curves, sported streamlined, body-skimming clothing and showed their arms, ankles and even their knees.

To accessorize their free-spirited look, the young lovelies of the time carried slim bags that wouldn't throw off the sleek lines of their silhouettes. A popular day bag was the Hermès Bugatti (after the racing car), which was the first handbag ever created with a zip! It was renamed Botilde after the car company sued in the latter part of the 20th century.

SIMPLE IN SHAPE, SUMPTUOUS IN DETAIL
The gorgeous interior of this hand-embroidered Garlands evening bag, circa 1923, is as opulent as its lushly decorated exterior.

HAND-EMBROIDERED EVENING BAG
This evening bag features the simple but chic chain handle and metal clasp that were so popular in 1923. A bag had to stay firmly closed during the Charleston!

" *I had no idea of originating an American flapper when I first began to write.* "

F. SCOTT FITZGERALD

EVENING WEAR
Delicate nighttime pouch bags were worn from the wrist. Jewellery was simple and delicate. Evening shoes (although similar to daytime styles) were made from luxurious fabrics.

DAY WEAR
The flapper's daytime wardrobe had the same basic elements as her evening attire. The handbag was larger and the overall look was completed with gloves and a cloche-style hat.

Tango purses and vanity cases

1924

Young women openly accentuate their assets with make-up. Everyone's favourite activity is dancing. Purses make it easy to have fun.

The 1920s were a decade of good times. Flappers and their boyfriends danced the nights away. While the Charleston was the era's most talked-about dance of the time, the tango was also popular, as were various other athletic dancefloor shimmies.

Made for dancing

Suddenly women needed handbags that stayed put. With their kicks, arm waves, bends and other big movements, the aggressive

dances of the day made it hard to hold a purse. To prevent a bag from being flung (accidentally we hope) from a wrist and into someone's face or body, a nearby punch bowl or the bandleader, certain innovations appeared. Bags

LADY WITH MINAUDIERE
Small bags were *de rigeur* in the 1920s. So much so that every female carried minaudieres and other mini bags. A good thing when you consider how out of place a big tote would be.

MINAUDIERES

A BAG FOR ALL
Plastic with an intriguing lipstick-hiding silk tassel, this exquisite vanity case is from France in the 1920s. The barrel-shaped bag could easily contain a few cigarettes, matches and whatever else a 1920s lady needed.

SMILE PLEASE!
An Art Deco, camera-style compact. This musical bag featured a winding mechanism allowing the bag to play a tune when opened. Just what an 'it' girl of the time needed.

got sleeker and smaller (palm-size was a favourite) with secure clasps (no drawstrings allowed!). Many were fitted with finger rings to secure the purse against the hand. Others featured short fabric handles or lengths of cord that could be wrapped around the wrist or hand. Anything that wouldn't fit in these compact bags was handed over to a date who would safeguard the items in his pocket. Aren't men just grand?!

Beauty bags

With the outpouring of cosmetics came the appearance of vanity cases. The smaller of these were what we 21st-century women would call compacts. Ornately decorated and holding only pressed

IRISDESCENT BEAUTY
This light-reflecting Whiting & Davis mesh bag draws approving looks from other females, and attentive stares from the menfolk. Or at least that was the theory.

face powder and a mirror, these often featured a metal chain and finger ring to keep them close at hand. Larger ones held powder, as well as rouge, a space for a lipstick, money and cigarettes. No girl worth her salt would be seen without a gorgeous case. Primping in public was a must-do among flappers. No one wanted to be caught with an ugly vanity case!

" Flappers — not for old fogies."

TAGLINE FROM FLAPPER MAGAZINE

MAD MONEY CARRY ALL
You name it, this bag may have it: a powder puff, a compartment for money with a built-in money clip, and a removable divider for coins. Check out the handy exterior clip. It's for a tube of lipstick!

Beaded beauties

Glass beads have been used on purses since the Egyptian times. However, the popularity of the beaded purse reached its zenith when 13th-century Venetians perfected the art of glass bead making, making it easy for more and more people to wear beads. Though these sensual beads were traded, sold and used as currency, many of them ended up on ladies' bags. And why not? For centuries women carried bags decorated fully or in part with beads. These bejewelled beauties were especially coveted by the nightlife-loving women of the jazz age.

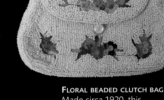

FLORAL BEADED CLUTCH BAG
Made circa 1920, this clutch is easily held in the palm. Or, slipped into a trustworthy date's pocket.

FINGER PURSE
It was popular at the time to carry bags that attached to the finger, hand or wrist. You could dance holding this one with no worries!

WRIST PURSE
This swingy number, a bit Art Deco in detail, features the juxtaposition of circle, triangle and rectangle, as well as several different textures.

Declutter your bag

Keep the inside of your purse organized to prevent damage and save time. Who wants to spend precious minutes each day digging through their bag for house keys or a pen? The best de-cluttering strategy: every evening go through your bag and throw away any rubbish. Place writing implements in a pencil case. Pare make-up down to the bare minimum and keep it in a make-up bag. Place keys, phone and other necessities in interior pockets. You're good to go!

It's easy to see why. Beaded bags are ornate, flashy and just gorgeous. They're the perfect 'look at me' purses. For flappers, that's just what the roaring 1920s were all about: attracting as much attention as possible. Whether they were made of thousands of glass beads hand-sewn onto linen purses or fashioned from flashy metal, these richly-decorated beauties reflected the light, giving them an intriguing sparkle. This was a time when the humble handbag became a work of art in its own right.

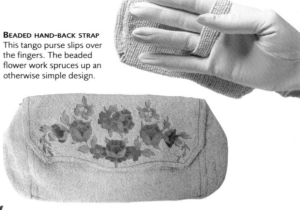

BEADED HAND-BACK STRAP
This tango purse slips over the fingers. The beaded flower work spruces up an otherwise simple design.

> " . . . in the form of beaded bags, the purse is reviving its former glories."

FASHION ARTICLE IN THE NEW YORK TIMES, *9 AUGUST 1925*

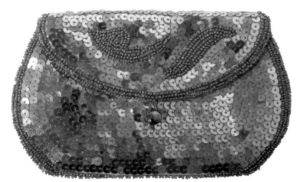

SEQUINNED AND GLASS-BEADED EVENING BAG
Lined in pale gold satin, this small bag packs a powerful flash. It features a small finger strap, allowing one to enjoy a dance and cocktail without care.

YASMENA BAG
From 2006, a modern take on the tango purses of yesteryear. This lovely purse is made by the popular Yasmena Handbags and is as convenient in the 2000s as it was in the 1920s.

Getting into gear

1925

Every 10 seconds, the Ford company completes a new car. Cars become more accessible and more affordable than ever before. And of course, you need a handbag for motoring!

The car played an indispensable role in shaping the Jazz Age. Back in 1925, many middle- and upper-income families were purchasing their first motor cars. Borrowing their parents' car gave younger people instant access to speed, freedom and fun. Yet the car changed more than leisure time – it also had an impact on fashion.

Most cars of the day were roofless or convertible. As a result, car coats and scarves became essential driving accesories. Capes

CAR AS ONE BIG MOBILE BAG
The car has always been a handbag of sorts, a ready place to stash all kinds of essentials and frivolous extras.

MUFF-BAG
This muff-bag keeps hands warm during a blustery drive. It also keeps essentials safely organized.

THE FLYING NUN!
This get-up is a face mask, designed to keep the face (relatively) bug-free. It folds down into a size compact enough to slip into a handbag.

with attached faceguards kept out dust and insects. Driving caps and goggles made you look the part, while day bags became larger and sportier-looking.

A bag to motor with

Muff-purses made a short-lived appearance. They allowed women to keep their hands warm and their essentials handy while riding in the passenger seat. Bags became heavier and sturdier to survive windy car trips. Picnics were a favourite car-centric activity and boxy bags were important in hauling supplies. Purses with mirrors or built-in compacts were necessary to touch up make-up and hair after a breezy ride.

CAR HANDBAG
This whimsical purse was made in homage to Ford's assembly line automobile. No one can accuse those flappers of taking their handbag style too seriously!

Handbag theft from cars

In the mid-1920s, handbag-from-auto theft reached epidemic proportions. Open-topped cars made it easy to scoop up whatever was in reach. The moral of the story? Take your bag with you! If you must leave it behind, lock it in the boot. Common sense is always the best defence.

" *They're all desperadoes . . . the girls as well as the boys.* "

FROM FLAMING YOUTH *BY WARNER FABIAN, 1923*

Art Deco

1927

Art Deco influences everything, from buildings to furnishings, art to fashion. To keep up, handbags become boldly shaped and decorated with strong colours and patterns.

Art Deco was one of the first important aesthetic movements of the 20th century. Rooted firmly in the world of visual arts, it embraced abstraction, distortion, simplification, geometry, bold contrasting colours and a celebration of technology.

The movement took its name from the 1925 *Exposition Internationale des Arts Décoratifs et Industriels Modernes*, held in Paris, which celebrated 'living in

ART DECO STYLE
Women wanted to look sleek, confident, aristocratic and so gorgeously capable. As this sleek clutch bag demonstrates, the right bag was essential.

the modern world'. Art Deco was for the fashionable set, the cool of the mid-1920s who were ready to put the prissy Victorian age behind them and embrace an aesthetic as fresh (and often as humorous) as their flapper sensibility.

ART DECO BAGS

BOLDLY SHAPED EVENING BAG
This swingy mesh purse has all the hallmarks of an Art Deco-era bag: a strong shape, a geometrical pattern and a certain sleekness. It combines femininity and impact to great effect

PRIMITIVE SWIRLS
Take a look at the design of a dozen Art Deco buildings and you're sure to see an aggressive, chunky pattern of swirls. This one, on an evening bag, reveals the face of a lion. Or is it a sun? A smiley face?

DELTA DECO
This triangular crocodile day bag is delicately understated, accented only by a short handle. The effect is exquisite, and this was a very streamlined bag to complement the fashions of the day.

ART AND GEOMETRY
This Art Deco lady is decked out in slim-fitting couture with dramatic geometrical patterns and contrasting colours.

The cult of the modern

To match the body-skimming fashions being created by designers such as Coco Chanel and Madeleine Vionnet, handbags became sleeker. In keeping with the movement's love of geometry, purse shapes grew bolder. Decorations included chunky swirls, zigzags and abstracts. High-contrast colour combinations, such as black-and-ivory, navy-and-white, were perfect.

"Get out! Get out! I am not dressing you!"

ART DECO FASHION DESIGNER MADELEINE VIONNET, WHENEVER AN AMPLE WOMAN DARKENED THE DOOR OF HER PARIS SALON

POUCHETTE CHROME FRAME ENAMEL BAG
Made in the early 1930s, this stunner boasts a classic Art Deco design of geometrical shapes and an eye-catching contrast of colours.

Happy days are here again!

1933

Hurrah! Prohibition in the United States finally comes to an end and the economy begins to recover from the financial mess left by the Great Depression. Time to celebrate in style.

BUCKET BAG
A popular style of the day, the bucket bag took off in the 1930s. This red leather example was made by Hermès.

All this good news put fashion designers in a celebratory mood. The day's silhouette was pretty, feminine and graceful – defined shoulders, nipped-in waists, slim skirts and great-looking accessories were in demand. In fact, 1933 was all about fun with accessories. Hats big or small, gloves for daytime, leather belts, narrow-toed shoes and the ever expanding handbag.

The popularity of shoulder bags

In the 1930s, women needed their hands free becasue more and more were employed in white-collar jobs outside the home. They couldn't travel to work holding a tiny clutch. Carrying a dainty reticule would make it difficult to take

GLITTER BOX BAG
This glittery bag features a strong shape and festive (but not gauche) finish – the ladies of the 1930s wouldn't have it any other way.

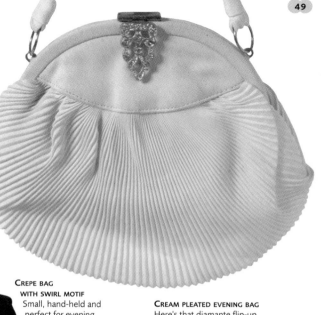

the bus to the office. These working women needed practical bags to stash their cosmetics, wallets, train tickets, notepads, writing implements and so forth. Shoulder bags were the perfect solution.

Elegance after hours

Women were seen at clubs, the theatre or fancy restaurants. They wanted gorgeous bags to match the gossamer evening dresses of the era. Dressy clutches and short-handled evening purses were made from crepe, silk and velvet, and were embroidered or pleated. Pretty jewelled clasps kept them tightly shut.

CREPE BAG WITH SWIRL MOTIF
Small, hand-held and perfect for evening. This embroidered bag has a rear handle for those ladies who can't resist a spin on the dance floor.

CREAM PLEATED EVENING BAG
Here's that diamante flip-up clasp again! And more crepe but this one makes a change from the classic black. Pretty, though. And great for after-hours socialising.

BLACK CREPE EVENING BAG
This pretty handbag is a tasteful, chic evening look perfect for the cocktail hour. The beautiful diamanté-decorated flip-up fastener is a 1930s clasp classic.

Meanwhile, back on the ranch...

The native people of the American Southwest are famous for their weaving skills. In the 1930s, as more and more of their reservations began opening up to tourists, native American artisans started to design beautiful and original souvenirs to sell to this new market. Blanket clutch bags were especially popular, providing a great option for casual weekend wear.

CLAUDETTE COLBERT AS CLEOPATRA
This French-born, American-raised beauty was a favourite of filmmaker Cecil B. DeMille. Her witty sexuality won her the part of the pharaoh queen in DeMille's 1934 epic.

EGYPTIAN CELLULOID FRAME EVENING BAG
A wonderful antique French-made, Egyptian-inspired evening bag, circa 1921. Created to celebrate the discovery of Tutankhamun's tomb, the bag has a soft velvet body and a celluloid frame decorated with an Egyptian-style cast of characters. The clasp is modelled on a pharaoh's head and, when pressed, opens the bag. History meets kitsch!

Pharaoh fashions

1934

Cecil B. DeMille's multi-million dollar spectacle *Cleopatra* appears in movie houses the world over. Suddenly everything is coming up pharaohs, and handbags are no exception.

'History's most seductive woman!' 'The screen's mightiest spectacle!' 'The love affair that shook the world!' With taglines like these, who could resist the movie *Cleopatra*? Claudette Colbert played the queen in all her sexy, glamorous glory. Women and men were mesmerized – if not by Claudette's performance, then by her cleavage-bearing Egyptian costumes.

Hoping to impart a sliver of cinematic style to their own lives, women snapped up the growing collection of Egyptian-themed furniture, house goods, clothing and accessories that designers were busy creating.

Handbags of the time were compact. Hand-held envelope bags were the most popular and were easily 'Egyptianized' with printed designs or embossed borders of hieroglyphic designs. For evenings, women favoured small chain-hung reticules with metal clasps.

EGYPTIAN LEATHER POCHETTE
This fun bag was produced in Egypt, where hundreds were sold to tourists as souvenirs. The discovery and unearthing of Tutankamun's grave in the early 1920s brought scores of curious Westerners to the land of the pyramids.

Designer bags

As the 1930s progressed, bag designers became more well-known. Some of the more popular designers included:

• Bienen-Davis. For the woman who preferred classic looks, the New York label's look was chic, urban and flawlessly constructed.

• Anne Marie of France made bags that looked like everyday objects.

• Elsa Schiaparelli was good friends with the great surrealists including Alberto Giacometti, who inspired her Big Apple pocketbook, and her use of animal prints, shocking fuchsia trim and abundance of mirrors.

CHAMPAGNE ON ICE?
This leather purse by Anne Marie of France, circa 1940, is the epitome of Surrealist chic.

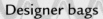

bienen-davis
NEW YORK

bienen-davis dramatizes "calf love" . . .
with the bright inventiveness, the fine simplicity,
and the masterly craftsmanship
that, with the little gold 𝖇𝖉 inside,
identify all bienen-davis bag originations

Surreal fashions

1935

Surrealism is at its peak. Designers adapt the movement to suit a variety of popular fashions, turning women into walking art exhibits and handbags into anything imaginable.

'Beauty will be convulsive or not at all,' said poet André Breton, the French leader of the Surrealist movement. No longer just for artists, writers and intellectuals, Surrealism began creeping into decidedly non-intellectual territory. By the mid-1930s, it had become a favourite theme of some of the era's more whimsical fashion designers.

Handbag whimsy

Surrealism provided the more fearless female with a range of playful purse options. It became more common to see ladies carrying bags shaped as body parts, various foods, telephones and more. Some of these designs were subtle – you had to look twice to notice a bag was shaped as a passenger ship. Some were so obvious as to be absurd.

ALL HANDS ON DECK!
At first glance, this French clutch bag from around 1935 looks like a fantastically made leather bag. Then you see that it is actually a ship replete with a trio of funnels.

TROMPE L'OEIL
This plain black canvas bag from Italy was painted to look like leather luggage by way of a design featuring straps and buckles.

EXHIBITION INVITATION
Surrealists from all walks of life united at the International Exhibition of Surrealism which was held in Paris on 17 April 1938.

The Hollywood Years

As the world battled through another war, Hollywood boosted spirits by putting a glamorous spin on the 'make do and mend' mindset of the time. Handbags may have been fashioned from inexpensive materials such as cloth, raffia or yarn, but they were functional and beautiful. With Dior's 'New Look' of 1947 and the voluptuous optimism of the 1950s, starlets as well as hoi polloi toted ritzier purses.

4

1940—1959

Make do and mend

1943

World War II rages on. Wartime rationing of leather, nylon, wool, rubber and other precious materials changes the look of bag design.

Yet another year of looking fabulous in nothing more than old dresses, re-tooled blouses and trousers sewn from bedsheets. It was also a year for innovative bags.

Gone were the traditional leather handbags. In their place were cloth sacks, drawstring pouches and shoulder bags. Yarn was knitted or crocheted into clutch bags. Fibrous materials, like straw and raffia, were whipped up into magical bags so stunning that even the Queen had one. No shame in conserving here! No, women of style knew that supporting the war effort was the ultimate fashion statement. Perhaps there's a lesson for us in this era of over-the-top designer bags. Is anyone ready to trade in her Gucci bag for a straw tote?

DOUBLING UP
This gingham drawstring bag may well have started life as a mere shirt sleeve

GLAMOUR AND GAS MASKS
Queen Elizabeth (later the Queen Mother) is pictured carrying both her handbag and gas mask after an official tour during World War II.

CIVIL WAR
Times may have been hard, but standards weren't allowed to slip. Even a felt bag can add to a colour-coordinated outfit.

SIMPLY RAFFIA-SHING
This shoulder bag was created from exotic raffia. It was clearly designed to stimulate happy conversation wherever the sun shines – on the beach or aboard ship.

Rational and beautiful

1945

Shortages and rationing force designers to be ultra-creative. Fortunately, they rise to the challenge, surprising war-weary women with styles that are both utilitarian and fanciful.

The year is 1945 and no woman with any common sense would dream of stepping out in public with a flashy, ostentatious calfskin bag on her arm. To do so would be risking dirty looks and mean-spirited comments from patriotic passersby. Carry a luxurious leather bag and one might even experience an 'accidental' jostle or trod-upon toe while shopping or waiting at the post office.

Handbags by hand

Ostentation, however, is something few ladies worried about in the mid 1940s. Whatever pretty leather bags these women may have once owned were surrendered years earlier to the armed forces to be refashioned into military uniforms. Thus, the average woman created her own handbag and ad hoc

BASKETS AND BAMBOO HANDLES
These two bags feature popular materials of the time. Either would look right at home today with a pair of jeans and a sweater.

"Waste helps the enemy. Conserve material!"

POPULAR WWII CIVILIAN SLOGAN

accessories from whatever material was close at hand: a decrepit wedding dress worn seven times, excess wool fabric from a shortened man's coat or maybe an army duffel bag from World War I.

CROCODILE BAG BY KORET
Koret was one of the era's favourite designers – and is much sought-after among collectors today.

Designer tricks

Some lucky women could afford more than homemade. For them, designers created utilitarian beauties such as canvas shoulder bags. There were drawstring satchels of velvet, satin or crocodile. Bamboo was sectioned into half-foot pieces and equipped with handles. Woven rattan was shaped into bags. All lovely ways to make do.

SACRED COW
Use your cowhide camera case as a handbag? Go for it! This look comes from a women's wartime magazine.

New hope, 'New Look'

1947

With WWII over, rationing comes to a gradual end. Claiming austerity is a thing of the past, Parisian fashion designer Christian Dior creates an opulent new silhouette.

In 1947, French designer Christian Dior created his first clothing collection. Tired of the severe, dreary days of post-war Europe, Dior wanted to brighten things up a little bit. Being French (and a designer) he turned his eyes to the ladies, giving them a 'New Look', complete with rounded shoulders, a cinched waist and skirts so voluminous that people were shocked. 'Sacre bleu! How much cloth did that dress take?' This was a total departure in fashion from just about anything that had gone before. As with many radical changes, reactions were polarized between acclaim and vilification.

CLASSY CLUTCH BAG
This small envelope bag is the perfect example of the neat bag of the era. The strong lines of the clothing – rounded shoulders and a cinched waist – give the look its strength. The role of this lady's handbag was to subtly blend in.

Essentials only

A compact handbag is only designed to contain the bare essentials. The slim clutches of the 1940s could not accommodate anything more than a small wallet and a lipstick and powder compact. Bags with delicate handles were intended for minimum daily paraphernalia.

Woo hoo! Something new!

Those ladies ready to leave the dreariness of the war behind saw Dior as a god. But not everyone was enthusiastic. The 'New Look' was radically different from the 'just long enough' slim-fitting skirts, dresses and jackets worn during the war. Some people carried placards denouncing the Frenchman, and essays were published espousing the thrift that had helped the Allies (in part at least) to win the war.

At least Dior's 'New Look' bags were tame. The billowy curves of his clothing were balanced with sleek, streamlined bags: clutches mostly, but also small square purses with short handles. They weren't very practical for working women, many of whom stuck with their roomier handbags.

FRANCIS WINTER FOR DIOR
This 'ballon' style bag was created in shiny red leather. Its curvy lines were the perfect complement to the billowy New Look style.

DIOR CLUTCH BAG
Another easy-going bag with not a lot of extra space, trim or anything, really. But stylish and the perfect counterpart to Dior's luxe, voluminous fashions.

> " *Zest is the secret of all beauty. There is no beauty that is attractive without zest.* "

CHRISTIAN DIOR

Bags and shoes

Whatever shape your handbag was, it had to match your shoes. With the 'New Look', coordinating became fun and competitive. Today's fashion followers wanting tips on tying a look together should visit 6pm.com to stay sharp.

Palinkas-Birot
BOTTIER · MAROQUINIER
15, RUE DUPHOT · PARIS 1ᵉ
TÉL.: OPÉRA 50.58

All that glitters

1951

The early 1950s are a time of sparkle, glitter and feminine fashion. After years of harsh rationing and making do, post-war women are ready to shop – for ultimate style.

Beauty was fashion's buzzword. Women were ready to spend the 1950s looking pretty. They also wanted to look their best for the young men back from the front line. Clothes were tailored, with soft shoulders, obvious bustlines, small waists and shapely hips. Bags complemented the gently sculpted style.

"She's beautiful – that's always interesting."

HIS KIND OF WOMAN (1951),
STARRING JANE RUSSELL

A VISUAL GOLD MINE
Jane Russell, wearing a gold-mesh evening gown, demonstrates the demand for glitz and glamour that was everywhere in the 1950s.

Right bag, wrong body?

Can a rotund woman carry a tiny purse? Can a teeny woman carry a vast tote? Of course! Just choose your bag with care:

• Broad shoulders, sturdy arms and large bosom: avoid short-handled shoulder bags that fall at the upper torso.

• Generous waist, wide hips: don't carry a handbag or shoulder bag that falls from the mid to lower torso.

• A large frame: do not carry a small bag, it will only make you look bigger. A medium to large bag with a tailored shape is ideal for you.

• A bony build: avoid skinny, long bags that will make you look awkward. Try something unstructured.

For day wear, the box bag continued to be a bestseller, followed by framed pouches in suede and calf. Shoulder bags in soft cowhide were in demand for casual wear, and for the autumn the large frame bag became popular.

Shine **on**

For evening inspiration, ladies looked to Hollywood. Favourite stars included Jane Russell, Ava Gardner and Marilyn Monroe. These tinseltown beauties favoured sequins, silk, satin, taffeta and anything else that glitters.

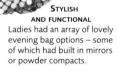

MATCHING BAGS TO GOWNS
Glamorous evening-wear styles demanded equally stunning bags. This gorgeous red bag is covered with glittering beads.

STYLISH AND FUNCTIONAL
Ladies had an array of lovely evening bag options – some of which had built in mirrors or powder compacts.

COCKTAIL HOUR
Small satin cocktail bags were all the rage. This cream satin bag has an embossed pattern and a delicate golden clasp.

Lovely Lucite

1953

Post-war technology leads to a high-class plastic called Lucite. In the hands of handbag designers, this highly adaptable synthetic is turned into the decade's hottest accessory.

Lucite is a brilliantly shiny, hard, firm, heavy, impossibly smooth material. Also called Perspex, acrylic glass or Plexiglas, it is an acrylic resin known in chemistry circles as polymethyl methacrylate. The celebrities, showgirls and society women of the 1950s, however, didn't care about any of this science mumbo jumbo. What mattered to them was that Lucite was gorgeous – especially when fashioned into the highly original, charming handbags designers were churning out.

Caring for Lucite

- Wipe away smudges with a damp sponge and, for stubborn stains, use a very small drop of mild soapy solution.

- Store far from sunlight, heaters and warm rooms.

- Don't store Lucite in plastic bags, which can discolour the material.

- Toxic fumes can form when Lucite is exposed to heat. Get rid of your bag if you smell fumes emanating from it.

Boxy beauties

Vanity case-style bags were especially popular, as were bags shaped like lunch boxes, beehives, hatboxes, ovoids, hexagons, clutches, as well as beaded or cloth bags with Lucite handles. Lucite was expensive, after all, and if you couldn't afford a whole bag, the handles would do! New York and Miami were Lucite handbag centres, with many of the

CARE TO DANCE?
This boxy beauty, circa 1950, is clear plastic decorated with Victorian ladies and gents twirling around the dance floor.

day's labels operating out of one or both of the American cities. Companies included Wilardy, New York (among the priciest and most coveted), Charles S. Kahn, Llewellyn (with their Lewsid jewel clasp and silk linings), Tyrolean (which edged its bags with metal filigree), Patricia of Miami, Leslie of Miami, Dorset-Rex, Dorset 5th Ave, Florida, Miami, and Rialto. As the 1950s ended, designers began making lower-priced bags with cheaper, lighter, less elegant and more breakable plastics. These bags were sold in five-and-dime stores and dramatically undermined the cachet of the original Lucite bags. As a result, status-needy ladies began looking around for the next high-end handbag.

SPRING HAS SPRUNG
An intriguing clutch-style, this bag features a flap of daisies and pansies. This item was made around 1958, right before the flower power fashions of the 1960s.

GET A HANDLE ON THINGS
This red crocheted raffia bag, circa 1950s, features a shiny clear Lucite handle and matching clasp.

IT'S IN THE BOX
Reminiscent of mother of pearl, this shimmery beauty boasts a quilted design on the lid. A gorgeous evening bag that could double as a vanity case.

" *So right whatever the occasion, wherever you are. . .* "

ADVERTISEMENT FOR
CHARLES S. KAHN LUCITE HANDBAGS

Beach babes

1954

War, what war? First world economies are thriving as consumerism takes off. With money in their pockets, people can afford to take holidays and listen to Elvis Presley.

SPOTS AND STRIPES
This sporty, spotty tote – in cheerful red and white – is by MM May, circa 1954.

Economically, the mid-1950s were a time of boom. Manufacturing and commerce had not only recovered from the second world war, but had rebounded with such enthusiasm that people could afford to buy and do more and more with their new lifestyles. Beach vacations and lolling about swimming pools became favourite leisure activities. Handbag designers created casual bags,

LONE STAR BAG
Crochet raffia handbag decorated with sea shells and silk flowers. Caron of Texas is a darling of the collector's set.

outdoor bags, and even beach bags designed to celebrate life in the sun. Some even teamed up with swimsuit designers to create coordinating purses. Girls buying new gear never had it so good!.

Fun in the sun

The era had strict unwritten rules about what bags to use with what. Generally speaking, Lucite or leather bags – even leather shoes – were not for the shore, nor the pool. Beachy materials were cheap but cheerful, designed for the coast: straw, raffia, canvas and other sturdy fabrics. To add an element of fun, which was deemed otherwise inappropriate for evening bags of the time, many makers decorated beach bags with embroidery designs, shells, images of flowers or beach umbrellas or other kitschy things. These totes were tantalizing, all about creating a good time.

Accessories, accessories!

The perfect purse was an integral part of a 1950s woman's total look. But there were other elements that came into play – even by the pool. Sunglasses, full make-up and chunky gold jewellery were all pool essentials.

ANYA HINDMARCH BAG
Though this sun-kissed number is from 2006, it perfectly celebrates the kitschy cool of 1950s beach culture.

BATHING BEAUTY
All dressed up for fun in the sun, this heavily made-up woman carries a bucket tote perfectly coordinated with her dramatic black swimsuit.

Coco Chanel and the 2.55

1955

Having made the shoulder bag a vital part of women's wardrobes, Mlle Chanel triumphs with the creation of her elegant 2.55 bag. An 'it' bag that remains 'it'.

Coco Chanel was famous for changing the way women dressed. Her little black dresses were best accessorized with a swipe of red lipstick, a golden tan, a sporty bobbed coif and plenty of stunning jewellery.

The innovative designer even changed women's handbags. 'I got tired of having to carry my bags in my hands and losing them. So I added thin straps,

THE ORIGINAL QUILTED BAG – THE 2.55
This luxurious leather bag, created by Mademoiselle Coco Chanel in 1955 was pure elegance, thanks to the sleek shape, logo clasp, and chain and leather shoulder strap. Magnifique!

so they could be used as shoulder bags,' explained the lady who found inspiration in soldiers' satchels. Her version, which was launched in 1929, was feminine and refined, made from black or navy jersey, and highly desirable

The birth of the 2.55

With time came changes. In addition to Coco's beloved jersey, the bag was made in silk (for evening) or

LUXURY BY CHANEL

BOWLING BAG
Chanel's 'Luxury' range for 2006 includes this fabulous bowling bag. Shown here in red calf-skin, it comes in three different sizes and a range of different colours and textures. The chain is incorporated into the bag.

SHOPPING BAG
One of the shopping bag designs in the range, this large black bag is not only gorgeous and very desirable, it is the epitome of style combined with practicality!

too, became flashier, and the introduction of brightly coloured leathers created a craze for buying a perfectly matched bag for every outfit. No more neutral coloured, one-bag-fits-all bags for this lucky bunch!

Late 50s luxuries

Accessories became more outlandish – hats of fur and feathers were all the rage, as were gloves and dark sunglasses, and stilettos so severe that women were asked to remove them before entering buildings. Luckily, fashionable women came prepared – those big, boxy handbags were often capacious enough to hold a pair of flat shoes, allowing women to change footwear into something more floor-friendly.

HOME STYLE
This rectangular handbag, made of woven straw, features a beautiful embroidered panel.

FABRIC FANTASY
This English fabric bag is decorated with an abstract pattern of muted colours. It is lined in cream satin and has a gold clasp.

WHITE MAGIC
A classic-shaped bag in white leatherette with a striking black satin lining.

THE 'IT' GIRL
Smart dress, circa 1958 – a slim suit, showy hat and smart bag in the year's most popular shape – the tailored tent with a clasp and easy-hold handles.

The Pop Years

Jackie O, beatniks, flower power, Mods and Rockers, glam rock, disco, early punk and Warhol's factory – popular culture of the 1960s and 1970s was about pushing limits. Music was frank and electric, art was larger than life. Fashion was heavily influenced by both. The chicest women favoured 'look at me' clothing reflecting the style of the decades' celebrities. No wonder handbag designers took their cues from the era's bold, way-out ways.

5 *1960–1979*

Love Leiber

John F. Kennedy's assassination marks the end of an era. Martin Luther King delivers his 'I have a dream' speech, John Glenn orbits the earth and the first heart transplant takes place.

From a fashion standpoint, the year 1963 appeared to mirror the 1950s. Women were still wearing white gloves, girdles and all manner of uncomfortable-looking fitted dresses, accessorized with zany pillbox hats and fussy handbags. To freshen things up, the Hungarian designer Judith Pietro

JUDITH LEIBER
The lady herself in 2001 and one of her beautiful bags. Stunning!

Leiber – married to American artist Gerson Leiber and living in New York – launched her eponymous bag company. The purses were just what ladies who lunch need: exquisitely crafted, large enough to hold necessities but not so big that they overshadowed a stylish get-up, and in styles and colours that were classic yet up-to-the-minute. Leiber carefully maintained her luxury image by selling her goods at only the classiest boutiques around the world. Owning a Leiber was like owning membership to an exclusive club, one which has included every First Lady since

STINGRAY HANDBAG 'JACKIE O'
The Stingray Handbag, also called 'Jackie O', was first designed in 1963. It proved so popular that it was reissued in the early 1990s.

"You don't have to put your whole life in your purse."

JUDITH LEIBER

Jackie O, nearly every NYC socialite since 1963, as well as fashion editors, actresses and models. But there were signs of change. Leiber's prices reflected the quality of her goods: in 1963 a chatelaine cost about $100. Today a Lieber bag can set you back $7000.

By 1965, hair was less coiffed and clothes were looser, shorter and more edgy. Brit Mary Quant symbolized the sexy, defiant mood of the mid-1960s with her minis, swing frocks, PVC fashions, plastic boots, and, a particular favourite, the clear Lucite handbag. Leiber's purses became showier. Enter the rhinestone-encrusted bags. According to Leiber, rhinestones were the only way she could think to salvage a shipment of ugly bags from her factory.

EVENING BAG 'SOCKS'
Made in 1990 and named after President Bill and Senator Hillary Clinton's cat, this whimsical bag is classic Leiber and similar to earlier work created throughout the 1960s, 70s and 80s.

The perfect cocktail

The cocktail has been around since the late 19th century. But it is the 1960s we most closely associate with these mixed drinks. Cocktail parties required special attire, including the perfect bag: small, easily balanced with a drink, oozing glitz, and perfectly set off by matching gloves.

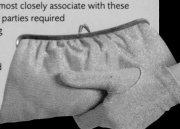

A passion for purses

1967

Cue the space race, race riots, hydrogen bombs and nuclear testing. The world is a-changin'. And yet it's never been a more important time to dress to impress.

One of those 'anything goes' years in fashion, if there was one unifying clothing theme to 1967, it was about being flash. Every woman, no matter what fashion tribe she belonged to, wanted her share of the attention. And she got it, with outlandish clothes, heavy use of gaudy jewellery, interesting shoes and 'look at me' handbags. Flower children had their handmade macramé, cloth, crocheted or suede numbers. Mods had their high-contrast, graphically

PSYCHEDELIC PUCCI
Pucci specialized in vibrant and colourful prints. This slim slip of a bag is dressed in the designer's signature swirly, paisley print. Far out!

VIVA LAS VEGAS
Fancy taking a gamble on this? This charming black souvenir bag features the names of a plethora of US casinos of the 1960s.

" Pucci largely invented the look of the woman of the moment — one might almost say he has invented the woman herself."

FROM A STORY IN AMERICAN VOGUE, 1960s

striking PVC bags. Printed bags were especially popular at the time: glamour girls, be they models, singers or actresses, went for Pucci or a fancy French designer name. Art students favoured anything kitschy. And those who didn't follow any particular fashion? They chose big straw totes, small dressy evening clutch bags, and other specialities of the 1950s. Truly, whatever style you went for worked.

STYLECRAFT BOX HANDBAG
Stylecraft, a US handbag maker, specialized in quality vinyl goods and is now much sought after. This bag, circa 1967, features an idyllic fishing scene.

Collecting tips

Like the decades that went before, the 1960s were filled with fun handbags that are now collector's items. Here are some helpful tips for snapping up a few of these bags for your own collection:

• Do your research. Found a bag you 'think' is a Pucci, a Stylecraft, an old Chanel? Study collector's sites online as well as collector's manuals to be sure. Beware the fake.

• If you're unsure about a bag's authenticity, contact an appraiser. Better safe than sorry!

• Look carefully at a bag's condition. Vinyl and other synthetics have a tendency to crack and warp if stored in heated or damp rooms.

MAGAZINE HANDBAG
So popular it resurfaced in the 1980s, this vinyl clutch bag looks a really good read. And it's just about big enough to fit a handbag in!

Gucci gold

1968

Gucci's shoulder bag is so often seen in the company of Jackie Onassis that it becomes known as 'the Jackie O bag'. Jackie continues to favour Gucci well into the 1970s and beyond.

Today one of *the* companies for must-have handbags, Gucci began life as a humble saddler when Guccio Gucci started making equestrian gear in 1906. By 1921, the brand was selling luxury leather goods out of a Florence store, and by 1938, a Rome-based store was selling handbags. But it wasn't until the early 1960s that Gucci goods entered the international public consciousness, thanks to highly aggressive expansion and Gucci's son Aldo's equally effective

EN VOGUE
Gucci announces its arrival in New York.

marketing – outfitting heavily photographed celebrities in Gucci, and creating a worldwide buzz. The company struck gold in the late 60s when Jackie Kennedy Onassis, America's First Lady of Fashion, favoured their designs.

DOUBLE 'G'
Gucci became known for its signature double 'G' logo as seen on this shoulder bag from the 1980s.

What do I have to do to get a bag named after myself?

Be glamorous: handbags do not get named after the unglamorous. Look your best at all times.

Befriend a designer: choose your favourite handbag – something distinctive – among his or her designs.

Wear the bag everywhere: take the handbag to parties where celebrities will be. Stand next to celebrities. Have photos taken of you, the bag and various celebs.

Think clever: wear the handbag in close proximity to *Vogue* editors. Keep an eye out for handy photographers.

Create a weblog: submit pictures of you and the bag to fashion weblogs.In your own weblog, refer to the bag by your own name to personalize it.

Have a Plan B: if all else fails, marry into royalty and star in a blockbuster movie – not necessarily in that order.

THE BOUVIER BAG
Gucci reworked the original Jackie O bag into a modern version for the 2000s known as the 'Bouvier'.

THE LADY HERSELF
Jackie Kennedy was rarely seen without her trusty Gucci handbag.

" The bitterness of poor quality is remembered long after the sweetness of low price has faded from memory."

ALDO GUCCI

Enid Collins

1969

For the young, the late 60s are about minis, go-go boots and love beads. The middle-aged find their own piece of fashion fun, thanks to a housewife named Enid.

What do the 1960s make you think of? Hippies, long hair, minis, ethnic fashions, sandals and suede fringed handbags maybe?. But not everyone was a flower child, and not everyone wanted to be seen carrying something suede or fringed. Ladies of tradition wanted something feminine and fun – but respectable, too. Enter Enid Collins.

A rancher's wife

Enid Collins was married to a struggling rancher. Needing to supplement her family's income, she created a small number of day bags to be sold in gift shops around her Texas home. Her most popular items were canvas bucket bags with embroidered and jewelled motifs, or painted wooden box bags. By 1959, Collins had opened her own store. Soon, she was offering kits for creative types who wanted an 'Enid Collins' at a discount.

BIRD IN HAND
One of Collins' most popular designs, this 1965 avian-influenced block of a bag is made of blonde wood. Collins initialled each one to ensure its authenticity.

What made her bags so special? They were solidly American but often with a safe nod to popular culture. And they were gorgeous, with quality construction, leather trim, paint, mirrors, sequins, crystals and popular natural themes.

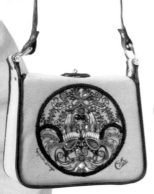

ELABORATE PATTERNED BAG
Another classic Collins bag: made of canvas with a leather strap, a brightly coloured motif dominates the design.

FLAMENCO HANDBAG
This bag is one of many imitations that appeared. In a gesture to genuine Collins bags, it features embroidered and jewelled canvas.

MADE OF MONEY
From 1965, this amazing painted money tree features rhinestone leaves and flowers festooned with gold 'coins'.

"For those who have a flair for the truly distinctive!"

ENID COLLINS SLOGAN

Hippy days
1970

Civil strife, love-ins and flower children welcome in the 1970s. Long hair, ethnic fashions and rustic accessories are all in at the turn of the decade.

A new decade had kicked off, but that seemed to pass many folks by. People were still fighting the same fights, chanting the same kinds of slogans, talking about the same issues and riding the same psychedelic-painted buses. Fashion trends, however, were all-encompassing and pretty much any look was in style. The cool mini skirts of the 1960s were still very evident but floor-length maxi skirts, floaty, dreamy dresses and thigh-high hotpants were imminent, offering a variety of different looks.

To go with their mini skirts and ponchos, hippy chicks of the early 1970s carried suede *anything* (the more fringe the better!), but cane-handled cloth bags and fabric shoulder bags were also popular. Girls went mad for tapestry purses, patchwork bags and wool clutches. The size of your bag didn't matter: the smallest purse sat equally alongside the heftiest bag.

ASCOT ATTIRE
Hotpants teamed with a small shoulder bag that didn't distract from the legs! Over-the-knee suede boots gave this look its jaw-dropping impact.

WOOL PURSE
This chic bag features a wrist strap, making it perfect for dancing or hands-free shopping!

FURRY NICE!
In the 1970s, anything went. Carpet bags were big. This fuzzy, fabric carpet-style bag swings on a delicate gold chain.

> " ...so we just came up with the word so you could ask us what bagism is, and we'd say we're all in a bag baby!"

JOHN LENNON

BODY BAGS

The year is 1969, and peace-loving Beatle John Lennon and his wife Yoko Ono are promoting bagism in Amsterdam, Netherlands. Bagism was a term created to satirize prejudice and stereotyping – by living in a bag, no one could judge you by your skin colour, length of hair, age or clothes. At least, that was the idea. Unsurprisingly, it never really caught on.

High fashion made by hand

Consumers placed a high premium on handmade anything – whether or not it was made at home. Magazines showed women how to make their own chic purses. Church ladies sold handbags at Sunday bazaars, while bohemian boutiques offered upmarket versions.

One of the most popular of the homemade-style bags was the denim

drawstring number, sewn from two squares of cloth and owned by nearly every American schoolgirl. Or, even more risqué, a pair of denim shorts, sewn shut at the legs, and completed with a strap. Voilà! A purse! Drawstring bags appeared in

PSYCHEDELIC MAN!
Carpet-style bags featured hippy patterns and added a carefree vibe to any outfit.

CANE HANDLES
This macramé bag features cane handles, a popular flourish through the late 1960s and early 1970s.

WHAT A GAYBAG
A fun little sac, in plastic mesh, from the intriguing-sounding company Martin Gaybag.

Are you a hippy?

You thought the hippy movement had died out? Think again. Answer these questions to expose your secret inner hippy:

• You say 'groovy', even though it annoys people.

• You wear or carry items of clothing made of macramé, or decorated with beads.

• You own a Bob Marley T-shirt.

• You love Native American, Peruvian or Indian things.

• You think tie-dye is cool.

• You wear some kind of band around your head.

• It doesn't bother you that your boyfriend never washes his hair.

• People tell you that you speak too slowly.

If you answered 'yes' to more than one of the above, there is hope: Get a pair of fishnets, a copy of Sex Pistols 'Never Mind the Bollocks', and a Birkin-style bag. And stop saying 'groovy'!

many guises: drawstring crochet
totes were everywhere, done up
in a wide range of groovy colours.
Basket bags were as popular as
ever and patchwork shoulder bags
(preferably in leather or suede) hung
on nearly every arm. And any
hippy girl worth her weight
in patchouli oil owned a
macramé bag – perhaps
worn together with a
matching belt and lots of
beads. It didn't take much
to be chic in 1970!

We're lost in music

1976

Folk, rock, glam, soul, disco, reggae and the burgeoning punk movement come together to create an anything-goes climate that affects everything from politics to fashion.

The mid-1970s was the original anything-goes era. Polyester, mood rings, prairie skirts, ponchos, wrap-around viscose dresses, stilettos, platforms, bondage pants, brothel creepers: with such a mish-mash of styles, looking chic could be a challenge.

Or, it could be ridiculously easy. Most younger women of the 1970s simply dressed to suit the music they listened to. And since there was such a wide range of musical styles around, dressing to fit in was easy.

Beyond the trend

Despise the handbags *du jour*? Try adopting elements of the current trend. Round chinchilla bags with pink handles all the rage? Choose a plain round bag with pink accents. Or, ignore the offending trend. If luxe croc bags are in, choose a wooden Enid Collins number adorned with a beaded butterfly. Or a Lulu Guinness number shaped like a birdcage. This way, you're blazing your own fashion trail.

TARTAN ARMY
Now here's a look: Bay City Rollers fans kitted out in the band's signature plaid and wear-everywhere print socks.

CHEQUERED PAST
Highland plaid was popular not only with the Bay City Rollers, but also with the punk movement, which was just emerging in the late 1970s.

Anything goes

Bay City Rollers fans wore plaid and three-quarter length trousers with strange socks. The appropriate bag? A cloth duffel or drawstring tote. New York punks wore battered T-shirts, ripped jeans, Converse trainers and the ubiquitous NYC messenger bag. Their UK counterparts dressed more flamboyantly in fishnets, bondage wear and creepers, and carried plaid handbags or household items, such as a tea kettle or lunch box.

ABBA fans and other disco divas stuck to wide lapels, filmy clothes and stilettos. Their perfect purse? A slim clutch bag or a small satin or tapestry bag on a metal chain. Earthy hippy

DIVA IN DEMAND
Throughout the 1970s, Barbra Streisand frequently graced the pages of *Vogue* and other fashion magazines.

girls slung brown leather or suede saddle-shaped bags over their shoulders. And ladies of a certain age? They held on to their Kelly bags and Le Sport Sacs for dear life!

"It's not a glamorous era."

BARBRA STREISAND IN A 1977 INTERVIEW WITH *PLAYBOY* MAGAZINE

PLASTIC FANTASTIC!
This fun, boxy bag is from the American cosmetic company Merle Norman – probably a gift-with-purchase. But its classic shape and strong neutral colours make it a perfect day bag.

DELILL GOLD BEADED BAG
Created by American bag designer Delill, who was famous for turning out tapestry, embroidered and bejewelled bags. This version, circa 1979, features a gold satin body festooned with gold, blue and pink glass beading.

The Designer Years

If there was one underlying theme in the 1980s, it was status. A French designer handbag, such as Chanel or Hermès, was the ultimate symbol of success. Trends changed in the early 1990s towards the label-phobic grunge style, where messenger bags and rucksacks ruled. Fortunately for handbag fiends, by the late 1990s sought-after sacs were back in vogue, and women were once again going potty for purses.

N° 5
CHANEL
PARIS

6 *1980–1999*

Money, money, money

1981

Margaret Thatcher, Reaganomics, the rise of Wall Street and big money. Celebrating the greed of the time were television shows like *Dynasty*, *Dallas* and *Falcon Crest*.

Money made the world go round, thanks to thriving economies throughout the western world. Jobs were plentiful. Women entered traditional male white-collar positions – from business school to brokerage houses – in huge numbers.

The shoulder bag

To get ahead in male-dominated fields, ladies played down their femininity, donning graceful versions of men's suits and low-key accessories, such as slim briefcase-like or saddlebag-shaped shoulder bags – a favourite of the 1980s career woman. Done up in black, cordovan or (more likely) navy blue, these hung from every self-respecting lady's shoulder.

ROSENFIELD PANTHER CLASP BAG
This is a simple envelope with an unobtrusive skinny strap. All is subtle with the exception of the over-the-top, gold-toned and rhinestone-studded clasp pushing the boundaries of good taste!

GET YOUR CLUTCHES ON ONE!

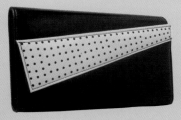

GOING DOTTY!
This slim envelope-style clutch bag has a touch of the New Wave that was *en vogue* at the time. Check out that dotty panel!

METALLIC GOLD AND JADE
This fun bag features the superfluous design elements (jade and gold 'rays') so beloved of the 1980s. The bag converts to a clutch by tucking the strap inside. Made in Italy by ZS Moda Denis.

In your clutch

The over-exaggerated fashion of the early 1980s was celebrated by shows such as *Dynasty*. Hair was enormous and clothes were in-your-face, done up in contrasting colours with imposing shoulder pads. Make-up was insanely obvious. How could handbags compete? By being clutch bags. Slim envelopes were ideal; they didn't distort the era's silhouettes nor did they add more to looks that did not need it.

POWER DRESSING *DYNASTY* **STYLE**
The high-fashion 'Joan Collins' style dress of the day: notice how well the slim clutch bag accompanies such a dramatic silhouette.

It costs what?

The 1980s may have been about making money, the 2000s are about spending it! 2006's priciest bags:

- Hermès crocodile Birkin (diamond clasp): $80,000.
- Hermès crocodile Birkin (regular clasp): $20,000.
- Hermès Birkin in leather: $8,000.
- Gucci crocodile shoulder bag: $14,800.
- Chloé Paddington crocodile satchel, $13,000
- Any Judith Leiber: Average $1,000–$6,000

> "*In my career, I've gone from babe to bitch to bag.*"

JOAN COLLINS, IN AN INTERVIEW WITH THE US MAGAZINE INTERVIEW

DIAMANTÉ RHINESTONE EVENING BAG
A black satin clutch bag covered in small rhinestones, this sparkler would look fabulous teamed with a big-shouldered sweater and slim pencil skirt.

GOLDEN ENVELOPE
Gold is the ultimate 1980s metal; it was nearly as beloved during the day as rhinestones. Here, it dresses up an envelope bag. It also boasts topstitching in the shape of a rainbow.

What's in yours?

What you have in your bag says just about as much as the bag itself. Take a look inside your everyday bag. Do any of the following sound familiar?

• A full cosmetic bag with facial cleanser, moisturizer, fingernail polish, nail file, perfume and hair styling products. You have a deep need to look a certain way, which may look nothing like how Mother Nature made you. Accept your looks and you won't need to carry so many cosmetics with you.

• Journal, sketch tablet, variety of writing implements, a book of poetry or meaningful prose. A creative type, always ready to catch an idea. Completely unconcerned with what others think.

• A mobile phone, Blackberry or other PDA, iPod, pager. You dislike silence, being alone, and feeling bored. Try a week without the gadgets, it may make you less needy.

• A manila folder filled with office paperwork. Yep, it's true, you're a workaholic. Stop looking so smug – there's nothing wrong with leaving work at work.

• A second pair of shoes, extra tights, umbrella, protein bar, sewing kit, tissue, bandaids, safety pins. Ready for anything, you also have a nurturing side.

Birkin: Birth of a legend

1984

Wanting a bigger, easier-to-handle handbag in which to carry her many things, British chanteuse Jane Birkin asks Hermès for help. The Birkin bag is born.

The Birkin bag's origins are shrouded in myth. One story has Jane Birkin on a plane sitting next to Hermès president Jean-Louis Dumas. Depending on reports, she was either carrying a straw bag complaining that it didn't fit everything inside, or a Hermès Kelly bag saying the bag's opening was difficult to get into. Other reports have Birkin being asked by Hermès to draw her dream bag. Whatever the truth is, the company made the bag and, say some sources, charged the performer $5,000 to purchase the finished product.

JANE BIRKIN AND HER BAG
Jane claims to own only one Birkin, although she could get another ... for a price. Hermès reportedly offers Jane a 10 per cent discount.

SARAH JESSICA PARKER
In 2006 Hermès closed the Birkin bag waiting list (which was several years long). An early episode of Sex & The City features character Samantha trying to bypass this dreaded list. Looks as if Miss SJ Parker may have been able to do just that!

THE NEW MUST HAVE?
'I love (my Hermès bag), but I lug so much stuff around in it I believe it is part of the reason I have tendonitis', said Birkin, in 2006 when she announced she was retiring her bag. 'Now I have a sporran. It's a delicious article that fits just the necessities'.

" I told Hermès that if I was them, I would seriously look into the possibility of creating a sporran."

JANE BIRKIN OF HER NEW FAVOURITE BAG, THE SCOTTISH SPORRAN

By Royal command

1985

With its distinctively British sensibilities and long history of service, Burberry nabs its second Royal Warrant, courtesy of HRH the Prince of Wales.

In the United Kingdom, the Royal Seal of Approval is the highest honour something can be given. Everything from services to consumer goods are eligible. The seal got its start back in the 1558 with protestant queen Elizabeth I. As a woman, a protestant in a country that had been catholic and the focus of various murder plots, she couldn't just trust any one. Those who were loyal received her special royal seal.

LASTING STYLE
In 2006, this saddle bag with Burberry's high-impact nova plaid, was a favourite with fashionistas and chavettes on both sides of the Atlantic.

GOOD MARKS
Quality handbag manufacturers, such as the British department store Derry & Toms, have been advertising their seals of approval for decades. This ad is from 1917.

" *A comb, a handkerchief, a small gold compact, and a tube of lipstick.* "

WHAT THE QUEEN, WHO IS NEVER SEEN WITHOUT A HANDBAG, CARRIES IN HER PURSE

Things have progressed since then and today, there are even royally approved handbags. Burberry was founded by gabardine inventor Thomas Burberry in 1856; it had originally supplied outerwear to Britain's armed forces and royalty and received its first seal – royal warrant – from the Queen in 1955. The second came from Prince Charles in 1989. Other handbag makers garnering prestigious royal warrants include Ettinger and H.R. Rayne. That's not to say royals didn't appreciate a good handbag when they clapped eyes on one. Favourites of the fashionable Princess Diana included quilted cloth totes Souleiado Sacs Magaridos, Tod's D Bag (which was named after her) and Globe Trotter hatboxes.

PRINCESS OF WALES
In her later years, Diana's favourite purse was Christian Dior's 'Chouchou' (My Sweet), given to her in 1995 as a gift by Madame Bernadette Chirac. In 1997, Dior renamed the bag 'Lady Dior' in honour of the princess. Incidentally, the bag's shape was inspired by a Louis XVI armchair that Dior admired.

Chavs of Cheltenham

Every country has them – functionally literate, underemployed, underclass white twentysomethings obsessed with luxury labels. In the UK, they're called Chavs (for Cheltenham Average, Cheltenham being the town where the name was coined). You'll find them in Reebok trainers, white t-shirts, gaudy gold-finished jewellery (and that's the men as well as the women), track-suit bottoms, Prada trainers, and plenty of Burberry check (real, or knock-off). You might think that this has affected the way people look at the luxury brand – perhaps it has, although execs at Burberry claim not to be worried one little bit. There's no such thing as bad publicity!

Designer backpacks

1988

Leave it to the label-obsessed 1980s to embrace a practical object made out of an everyday material, and turn it into the period's most coveted status symbol.

In 1985 Miuccia Prada, granddaughter of Prada founder Mario, slapped a Prada label on a backpack. Not just any backpack, but one with a clean, attractive silhouette. A nylon backpack. A type of nylon Miuccia called Pocone. People have been using rucksacks for decades to carry supplies, camping equipment, sporting goods, even to lug books to and from school. What made Prada's version different was it was small. And light. And it was meant not for heavy-duty schlepping, but to replace a woman's purse.

FURRY PACK
This rucksack features a main strap that unzips into two shoulder straps.

BY VIRTUE OF VUITTON
One of several designers to hop on the designer backpack wagon, Louis Vuitton's sportiest rucksack is its Monogram Montsouris.

Designer rucksacks

Originally priced at around £250, Prada's Vela was seen on the arms of stars like Jerry Hall and packs of supermodels. By 1988, not only had Prada's line expanded, but a thriving trade in illegal faux Velas had sprung up to meet the demands of those who couldn't afford the genuine article.

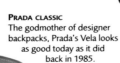

PRADA CLASSIC
The godmother of designer backpacks, Prada's Vela looks as good today as it did back in 1985.

Protect your wares

It may be only a backpack, but if it costs hundreds of pounds, it's important to treat it like the investment it is. Here's how to keep your purchase in great condition:

• Make sure your hands are clean before touching your bag.

• Don't set your bag on kitchen counters, the ground, or anywhere else that may have oil, dirt or chemical residue.

• Don't overstuff it! You risk weakening seams, stretching leather or fabric, stressing zips or other closures, and ripping the lining. Not to mention distending the straps.

• For short to long-term storage, place your bag in the original dustslip (if it came with one) or in a white cotton pillowcase.

• Place pens, make-up, bottles of water and anything else that can spill into plastic bags to eliminate damage to your bag's lining.

• Keep authenticity cards. Some designers require these before doing repair work.

• Check manufacturer's care instructions before attempting to clean the bag yourself. Some materials can be ruined even by using just plain water.

Kate Spade

1993

A time of 'anti-fashion', the early 1990s are minimalist and utilitarian, marked by grunge and a penchant for retro clothing. Women patiently await good-looking handbags!

In the early 1990s, handbags weren't the big deal they are now in the 21st century. Though there was the random Birkin or Chanel bag, the majority of women carried something black or brown, usually mid-sized, typically a shoulder bag kind of purse. It simply wasn't a big handbag time – and the market bore that out. Looking for something fun to carry, New York-based Kate Brosnahan (then a magazine accessories editor) and her boyfriend Andy Spade (comedian David Spade's brother) got to work. Kate was preppy, girly, with an innocent, unslick fashion sensibility. Her desire? A small line of handbags that were fashionable but not trendy, fun but not gaudy and timeless without being boring. The result was a well-edited line of six carryall-style handbags. With their

KATE SPADE
née Brosnahan, married Andy Spade in 1995. Here, she wears a typical girly, retro-preppy get-up.

" I've never thought of style as something you invent, like trying to come up with the proverbial better mousetrap. I think style is part of the way we live . . ."

KATE SPADE FROM HER BOOK STYLE

strong box shape and clean, interesting lines, the bags were made in an unexpected material – satin-finish nylon. As the company grew, other materials and shapes were added.

Small bag, big deal

Kate's bags took New York by surprise, capturing the hearts of women who couldn't afford anything French, but wanted to carry something better-looking than the depressing lower-priced purses available at the time. Soon, the bags were becoming an international

LUCKY LOHAN
This 'Annemarie Tripoli', calf hair handbag with its zany animal print and classic boxy shape, is the same one celebrity Lindsay Lohan purchased in January 2006 for $695.

Girlie vs. Grunge

1993 was the year of grunge. As Seattle-based grunge musicians such as Pearl Jam, Nirvana, Hole and Sound Garden earned US – then international – attention, their clothing styles were copied by fans. This meant layers of inexpensive (often thrift shop) clothing, these were struggling musicians, after all. Long underwear, concert t-shirts, flannel shirts, hooded sweatshirts, bandanas or ski caps for heads, jeans, tube socks and weatherproof Doc Martens were all in style. Handbags were almost non-existent. Instead, boys and girls carried canvas messenger bags and backpacks. Very different from the aesthetic being pushed by Kate Spade!

phenomenon. Originally $155, Kate Spade bags were ideally priced for females hungry for the status of some kind of label. A favourite with urban workers in creative fields such as publishing, public relations, advertising and marketing, it soon seemed as if every hip woman carried a Spade. (After all, the bag went with everything, but wasn't so mild as to disappear into an outfit.) Wanting to get in on Kate's action, a flood of copycat bags hit the market. Somehow that made the genuine article more desirable.

Tassenmuseum Hendrikje

1996

Hendrikje Ivo, a Dutch handbag collector, brings together her collection of over 3000 handbags. The Tassenmuseum Hendrikje is founded in Amstelveen.

A personal passion for handbags led former antiques dealer Hendrikje Ivo to amass thousands of high-quality, quirky, rare and wonderful bags. The historical, social, artistic, even feminist implications of the bag, as well as the great variety of shapes, materials, ornamentation and techniques used all fuelled Hendrikje's passion. But

THE TASSENMUSEUM
An Aladdin's cave of handbags awaits behind those doors! The museum moved to Amsterdam during the summer of 2006.

PAPIER MACHÉ
Made from paper with a cut steel frame, this magnificent bag, *circa* 1810, comes from France, where ladies know a thing or two about the power of the purse.

what to do with so many purses? Give them their own building, of course! And in 1996, that's just what Ivo did, in the form of Tassenmuseum Hendrikje, the largest museum of handbags and purses in Europe. With its range of early bags, The Museum of Bags and Purses charts the development of handbags from the late Middle Ages to the present day.

EXOTIC RETICULE
This beauty features leather, tortoiseshell and mother of pearl.

For safekeeping

True, you probably don't have 3000 handbags to worry about, but even a small collection needs to be stored carefully to keep it in tip-top condition:

• Undo straps and buckles to avoid indentations.
• Clean gently according to manufacturer's directions.
• Store bags in a dark place (sunlight causes damage).

The ultimate collection

The Museum of Bags and Purses features a huge selection of 16th and 17th century pouches and purses; 18th-century pockets, letter cases and framed bags; 19th-century reticules; and a great variety of bags from the 20th and 21st centuries. The museum also holds surreal bag styles, including a ship, a

> " *Everything I need is right here in this extraordinary purse.* "
>
> DOROTHY KILGALLEN, AMERICAN ACTRESS

magazine, and a house. There are bags that have belonged to royalty, examples of modern classics, and all kinds of designer bags, including a bag that belonged to Madonna. And last but by no means least, is the museum's handbag shop. Filled with unique modern bags, it's a great place to find a handbag that no one back home has.

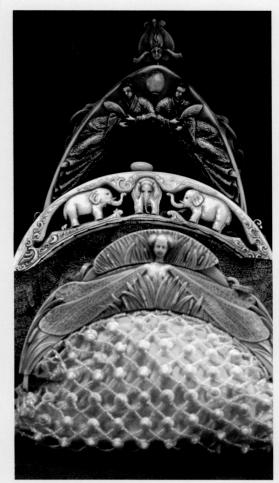

PLASTIC FRAMED BAGS – THE SURVIVORS
It is amazing that these gorgeously ornate plastic purse frames have survived into the 21st century. Careful storage is the key – especially for fragile materials so vulnerable to heat and light changes.

LEATHER BAG BY LEDERER
A high-sheen tailored box of a bag made in the 1950s. Think how it could dress up a pair of jeans and ballet flats!

Loopy about Lulu

1999

Tired of look-alike, high-status handbags, a former model turns her attention to fanciful purses. The novelty bag is born, perfectly capturing the spirit of late-century UK style.

Lulu Guinness began her career as a model but always wanted to create handbags. She decided to follow her dreams in 1989 and by 1996 her shop in Notting Hill was attracting loyal customers such as Madonna and Jerry Hall. As her business became more successful, Guiness relocated in 1999 to larger digs just off Sloane Street in London's shopping central. Soon after, outposts in NYC's West Village

(2001) and in West Hollywood (2002) opened. The buzz was growing!

House bags

Among Guinness' first commercial successes were her House Bags, a high-priced collectible series of

LULU GUINNESS
The beautiful queen of the novelty bag: Lulu Guinness.

HOUSE BAGS

ORIGINAL HOUSE 1995
This charmer is hand-embroidered in black satin and features a cherry red roof.

SHOP 1997
Done up in Lulu's signature lilac and cream, this bag features a handbag shop front. A must for the handbag fanatic.

PARISIAN HOUSE 1999
Deep lilac with a black roof, this charming home, er bag, comes decorated with embroidered flowering vines.

whimsical canvas handbags in the shape of houses, shops, theatres and huts. She leaned heavily on her favourite colours – lilac and cream – adding appliqué, embroidery and other subtle touches.

Signature style

From the start there was a certain allure to Lulu's irreverence and witty retro chic. The bags, however, were equally appealing; novelty bags shaped like various unexpected things from everyday life – buildings, body parts and pieces of clothing all having a delightful charm about them.

FLORIST'S BASKET *circa* 1993. Made of black satin with red suede roses, this is one of Lulu's first bags.

BEACH HUT This adorable canvas bag features embroidery and appliqué and is finished off with shiny red handles.

THEATRE 2002 Deep red curtains are drawn to show a special performance. This bag's decoration even depicts an audience.

The bags were often decorated with Lulu's witty bon-mots ('Dare to be Different', 'The World is Your Oyster'). Anyone with a Guiness bag would certainly stand out from the crowd!

Other bags

The bag that started the designer's ascent to stardom was a not-so-simple bucket bag – shaped like a florist's bucket and topped with roses. Other bucket-styles soon followed, including bouquets, plants, and even, yes,

CHOCOLATE BOX 2002
This limited edition chocolate box is a lilac moiré bucket bag with gold trim and felt chocolates. Delicious!

The bag lady

In 1998, French artist Nathalie Lecroc began work on her *Anthologie des Sacs*, a collection of watercolours depicting the contents of real women's purses. And no careful editing is allowed! The artist charges 300 francs for her services, which include emptying your day bag of its contents and creating a collage of them. The process can take up to three hours, depending on a woman's haul. And from this, Lecroc analyzes you. The collection is scheduled to be published after the insides of the 1001st sac is painted.

chocolates! Next came lips, wings, shoes and corsets, nothing was too far-out for Lulu – or her fans. Her clientele grew to include Elizabeth Hurley, Dame Judy Dench, Helena Bonham Carter, Björk, and Katie Couric. As Guinness' fame grew, so did her product line. Joining the novelty collectibles were laminated totes, day bags, evening bags, coin purses, cosmetic bags and even baby-changing bags. Some were staid in shape with eccentric touches – lip-print fabric or appliqué poodles. Others were even more bizarre: faux snakeskin lips in red, gold or silver.

> " *Sometimes a well-dressed man is the best accessory* "

FROM GUINNESS' BOOK, PUT ON YOUR PEARLS GIRLS

RED SNAKESKIN LIPS
Think of the pick-up lines you would get carrying this! Fashioned in bright red, this clutch bag is only for those who want to be spoken to.

ROYAL APPROVAL
On a 2005 visit to the Museum of Modern Art in NYC, Camilla, Duchess of Cornwall, shows her UK pride with the Flag Felicity Purse, a limited edition, sequinned Union Jack bag designed in collaboration with British artist Ann Carrington.

What else?

The early 2000s have been busy for Guinness – a book entitled *Put On Your Pearls Girls*, inclusion in the Victoria and Albert Museum, a stunning retrospective at NYC's Sotheby's and new bags. For those who love Lulu, but can't live without a classic leather bag, two more high-end ranges joined the Lulu line-up. Out for Autumn 2006 – the couture collection of Italian leather, calf and suede bags, and a range of leather vanity cases.

STAMP FRAME BAG – ARTIST'S LIMITED EDITION
Like the Flag Felicity Purse, this was created with artist Ann Carrington, who originally thought up the design in homage to the British postage stamp. The image is made from hand-sewn pearl buttons and makes this a very vibrant bag.

The Shape of Things to Come

Almost every week another celebrity introduces a handbag line and a new bag trend appears. People are talking about bags everywhere – on blogs, on websites, in newspapers and magazines, on the TV. In response, bag prices skyrocket. Fortunately, so do the number of ways to obtain a luxury bag, from online auctions to rent-a-purse services. Handbag lovers of the 2000s will not be denied!

7 *2000+*

Paul Smith

2001

Iconic and oh, so British, designer Paul Smith is knighted on 24 November, 2001. Later the same day, he marries his long-time business partner – Pauline Denyar.

In 1970, Paul Smith opened his first London menswear shop, specializing in suits. These were not just any old suits, but high-quality Anglo-style suits modernized with pastel shirts, striped pocket squares, floral ties and unexpected touches. Young followers of fashion couldn't get enough. The men's designs were so successful that women's wear was a natural next step. And you can't have women's wear without handbags.

A genius who merges the unexpected with the everyday, Smith's bags were based on classic shapes but featured unusual touches (such as extra pockets) or surprising materials. Smith's solid exciting and modern designs have won him countless accolades over the years.

NEW YET OLD
A modern purse shaped like a classic bowling bag. The twist is the carpetbag fabric decorated with various flora and a large country mansion.

" I give classics just a little kick "

DESIGNER PAUL SMITH

SWIRL STYLE

EAST-WEST SWIRL
This roomy purse in Paul Smith's signature swirl is everything to everyone. Its simple and practical boxy shape complements the multicoloured curved stripes. A Paul Smith classic!

A MODERN MATCH
You've heard of matching handbags and shoes? Go a step further and wear the same print on your arm and your feet with this set.

PRACTICAL CHIC
A Paul Smith handbag with side pockets and charm buttons in black embossed leather. The whimsical strap is a combination of printed swirl canvas and black leather.

POCKET X3
Pink pebbled leather dresses up this striking bag that is a bit boho, a bit sleek, and very modern. An unusual touch is the top...it's a drawstring

Glitz and glamour

2002

Bling is the word as fashion takes simple shapes and loads them up with colour, buckles, metal, skins, beads, sequins, and other eye-catching stuff.

Another year, another trend. In 2001, sleek clutch-style shoulder bags were all the rage. Everyone from Lulu to Luella offered a version. And why not? These classically-shaped bags were chic and classy, the perfect thing to wear with the feminine fashions of the time.

Bring it on

There was one big difference, however, between fashion before and the looks appearing in 2001: Bling. This was the year of piling it on. Brooches were big, hair ornaments were a must, belts were a go. Necklaces and

KAREN MILLEN The high street fashion chain takes a petite bowling-style bag, *circa* 1999, and updates it with snakeskin and metallic leather.

Putting on the glitz

Everyone should own one spectacle of a bag. Whether a gilt Brazilian sac fashioned from ring pulls (like this one from The Bag Queen) or a beaded clutch. Just be sure the rest of your get-up is decidedly un-twinkly. You don't want to look like a Christmas tree!

earrings, rings and bangles? Yes, yes, yes and yes. Of course, handbags that year followed what everything else was doing. Thus, a perfectly classic envelope-like clutch with a simple chain or leather shoulder strap was covered in baubles. Some had rhinestones. There were metallic accents and iridescence. And women, being the good sports they are, adapted beautifully. After all, once in awhile it's fun to play dressing-up.

DIESEL BAGUETTE
Keeping in line with the bling looks of 2001, this slim clutch-style handbag features a simple shape and bejewelled finish.

FENDI BAGUETTE
Well, yes, it is a designer purse, but this clutch-style shoulder bag by Fendi is glitzy in the extreme. Brown logo leather, iridescent blue reptile skin clasp AND red and blue beads.

Animal magic

2003

Fur, anti-fur, bags for animals, bags with animals, bags with the skin of animals, bags for animal charities. The year 2003 is all about animal magnetism.

The history of handbags and animals are closely intertwined. Leather and other animal skins such as wool, silk and furs have been used in the development of purse making.

Furry friends

Many fashion designers and editors call 2003 the year of the fur. A trend towards animal hair, as well as exotic skin, created a huge hairy demand in some circles. One

DOGGY BAG
The classic German Shepherd carries an equally classic envelope-style shoulder bag. Around his neck, of course.

unfortunate result of this: the death of endangered animals for their skin. According to the Convention on International Trade in Endangered Species (CITES), in July 2003 alone, Chinese officials impounded 1,276 illegal pelts, including the skins from tigers, leopards and otters.

Groups such as People for the Ethical Treatment of Animals (PETA) spent the year staging countless protests against the trend. Fortunately, smart fashionistas found a gentler, way to wear animals: in the shape of handbags. Or, as images on handbags.

BAGS FOR DOGS
This carrier by Millie and George is great for those who don't make their dogs walk.

LAP DOG BAG
Lulu Guinness turns the handheld clutch into a fluffy black chenille pooch, with a red and white bow.

A dog in the bag

Animals weren't just a form of handbag decoration, they were accessories in themselves. As the miniature dog trend exploded (thanks to all those super models with their tiny dogs), dog carriers went upmarket. Designers from Vuitton to Lulu Guinness added a dog bag to their lines, while dozens of others began churning out their own fashionable canine carriers.

BIRDS OF A FEATHER
This pale green bag features a bold birdie appliqué in pinks, purples and golds.

LAZY COWS!
The four-legged ones, of course. A bold bovine peers in on two sleepers on this Anya Hindmarch tote, from her line of monochrome photo printed bags.

KITTY GALORE
This pink, be-charmed lovely is a testament to the power of feline prettiness. The cutest way to carry your change around. Purrfect!

BELONGS TO BUNNY
Another Anya Hindmarch tote, done in a pastel print and decorated with an image of a little white bunny.

Anything goes

2004

Gwen Stefani attends the Grammys with her customized Le Sportsac. Her 'anything goes' love of colours, textures and shapes celebrates this year's mix-it-up style.

Backtrack thirty years earlier to 1974 – the only unifying fashion themes seemed to be shades of brown (chestnut, mahogany, tan, khaki, buff) and the wildly successful launch of the LeSportsac line of totes, bags, clutches, and travel bags. No matter where you travelled, you would see LeSportsac – hanging from the shoulders of pretty young things, nestled among the shopping

bags held by a 1970s suburban mum, even tucked under the arms of older sophisticates. Made of ripstop nylon, these were utilitarian enough to charm even the 'earthy-crunchiest' of 1970s fashionistas, yet 'French' enough to delight high society matrons. After decades of being overshadowed by expensive labels, LeSportsac made a splashy comeback in 2003 when stylish singer Gwen Stefani helped design a line of 'rock sacs' for the

DARE TO BE DIFFERENT
Have a peep at this! This irreverent bag is pure kitsch. Not for the faint or frigid, the swingy heart is emblazoned with a sexy lady sitting around waiting for something to happen.

SHE WAS A HOLLYWOOD CALLGIRL

PEEP
THE SAUCIEST GIRLS IN TOWN

LESPORTSAC FUN

TRIBECA TOTE
This roomy bag, available in a choice of different plains and prints each season, is a bright blast of cherry colour. The strong tailored shape is the perfect balance to bold patterns.

CITY SATCHEL
A LeSportsac classic, this satchel is a great gym or yoga bag, perfect as a hip baby changing bag, an ideal beach tote and great for carting wine and snacks to a picnic. Available in an ever-evolving range of prints and plain colours.

Carrying a quirky bag

Maybe it was shaped like a pair of lips, or came plastered with naked ladies, or was fabricated of fake turquoise monkey fur. At one time or another, most of us have fallen victim of an amusing purse. Sure, these wild accessories are fun, but if you don't know how to wear them, they can be detrimental to your style. In order to look cool when toting a kitschy bag you need to keep the rest of your get-up low-key. No feminine tuxedos or spangly jackets. Unless you're really fearless, stick to casual situations – a wacky bag doesn't work with your Sunday best. If your hair is big, make it small. Big hair and an amusing purse are so 1980s. Finally, if you're over 25, avoid anything with *Hello Kitty* on it at all times. Please!

'LE FAB' GWEN STEFANI
The L.A.M.B. lady herself, shown here at the 2004 Grammys carrying a text-heavy LeSportsac clutch of her own design.

THE 'STELLA'
A classic handbag, streamlined and so smart. This tailored purse is great with a sundress, a little black dress, an office suit, cocktail attire. Shown here in an airy, lighthearted print.

brand. Stefani's LeSportsac line, dubbed L.A.M.B. (the name of her childhood dog and the acronym she uses for her own fashion line), began when LeSportsac got the idea of asking her if she'd like to be a guest designer. Gwen got to choose prints and colours for various bags. And continued to do so for four seasons. Suddenly, everyone is carrying a Le Sportsac again.

HIGH STREET 'BOHO'
A big, robust bag, this roomy canvas number features sturdy leather straps and an intriguing array of ... buttons.

BOWLING BAG
You don't have to be a bowling devotee to yearn for a bowling bag! The classic bowling shape is trendy and practical .This pink number with dove grey lion and trim is by Pringle.

Something for everyone

Once in a while, a year comes along in which fashion is so all-encompassing, so democratic, that women are left scratching their heads ... or throwing on whatever they want. 2004 was just such a year. LeSportsac wasn't the year's only handbag trend for purse lovers. Everything went, from bowling bags to slogan totes, messenger bags to beaded reticules, straw bags to designer clutches. There were a few small micro-trends, however. Big was beautiful – bags were at least large enough to house a pair of trainers and a fully-stocked cosmetic case. Metallics were creeping into vogue, as was fur (real and faux), which was stuck randomly

SEVENTIES STYLE
A soft blend of green ovoids dress up this carpet tote, which features tan leather bottom and straps. This is another example of a larger bag to sling everything in.

LIZ CLAIBOURNE
This pink, black, and cream bag shows off one of the year's trendiest colour combos. The textile purse features removable straps for those times when you'd prefer a clutch.

on bags without any thought as to how odd it looked. Cloth was popular. Boho-chic, too, was important, as women embraced the gypsy-hippie-arty idea espoused by trendsetters like Sienna Miller and a softer, earthier Gwyneth Paltrow.

" . . . the handbags and the glad rags that your grandad had to sweat so you could buy . . . "

JON ENGLISH, AUSTRALIAN MUSICIAN AND PERFORMER

Man bags

Don't call it a purse! Urban men who don't have cars in which to stash their daily necessities, now carry messenger bags, sling bags, upmarket rucksacks and other masculine carryalls. Actor Jake Gyllenhaal has been photographed several times wearing a sleek androgynous bag slung over his back. Labels across the spectrum have brought out an array of man bags so heavy in testosterone that no one would dare mistake them for purses.

ANNA SUI
New York's downtown diva shows fabric totes, perfect for stuffing with all kinds of, well, stuff.

"*If I weren't so beautiful, maybe, I'd have more character.*"

Handbag wars

2005

Purses replace shoes as fashion's object of lust. Suddenly, everyone from B-list celebrities to near-dead fashion houses are making an upscale, highly covetable bag.

The price we pay for style! As handbags become a more important (or at least scrutinized) part of a woman's wardrobe, prices go up, fakes flood the market, waiting lists are established and women max out their credit cards trying to keep up with what the celebrities are carrying.

The price of exclusivity

It may well have been the year of the handbag, but 2005 was also the year of exorbitant prices. Let's face it, designer bags have never been cheap, but this year American retail analysts reported a 15 per cent increase in handbags. An example: The popular Prada leather bowler bag was about £450 when it was introduced in 2000. In 2005, it cost about £800.

New makers flooded the market, trying to capture a piece of the high-end purse action with bags that cost £500, £1000 and more. Still, everyone wanted a high street bag! To meet the demand, replica bag makers and counterfeiters were as busy as ever, churning out lookalikes that were close enough to appease the fashionista of average means.

I want one... NOW!

The turn of the 21st century was a great time to be a handbag lover. So many choices! All so gorgeous! But it was a rough time too, what with exorbitant new pricing and waiting lists so long that many design houses began shutting them. But women always find a way to get what they want. In this case, eBay. With a quick click, you could have a secondhand designer bag or – the cheapest option – a replica bag. Designed to look just-close-enough to the real thing, the best replicas were openly marketed as copies, thus avoiding all that ugly, illegal, counterfeit business.

I DEFINITELY SAW IT FIRST!
Females have been arguing over designer bags for decades. Here, 1970s supermodels Jerry Hall and Marie Helvin battle over a Burberry. Helvin looks the stronger of the two (just look at Hall's tiny arms!); we wager she'll get the bag.

Oprah and Hermès

Did you hear the one about Oprah? She walked up to the Paris Hermès store 15 minutes after closing time and asked to be admitted but was turned away. The incident, in June 2005, quickly escalated to name-calling. 'Racist,' spat Winfrey's supporters. 'Self-entitled! Too big for your britches! Show-off,' yelled others. 'We were closed – and getting ready for a private company event,' explained Hermès.

In an attempt to clear things up – or shame Hermès – Winfrey devoted an episode to the incident. Her guest was Robert Chavez, the CEO of Hermès USA. 'I would like to say we're really sorry,'

Chavez told the star. 'You did meet up with one very, very rigid staff person.' 'I just want to say shame on anybody for thinking I was upset for not being able to get into a clothes store and buy a purse,' said Oprah. Phew! Now that's settled, we can all feel good about pining for that Hermès bag.

> *" Oh honey, it's not so much the style, it's what carrying it means!"*
>
> SEX AND THE CITY'S *SAMANTHA,*
> ON THE ALLURE OF THE HERMÈS BIRKIN.

CHLOÉ PADDINGTON BAG
One of the hottest, most lusted after bags of 2005. Could it be the boho slouchy shape? The tough-looking handles? The padlock?

MULBERRY PHOEBE BAG
The saddle-shoulder bag that everyone was willing to pay from more than £600 for. Also popular: Mulberry's Joni bag.

The 'IT' bags of 2005

2005 was the year it was *de riguer* to carry a big name bag. Many of the year's favourites came from long established handbag labels. Think Vuitton, Chanel, Gucci, Coach, Bottega Veneta, Fendi, Hermès. But new favourites emerged as well, including Alexander McQueen's Novak – an homage to actress Kim Novak. With the exception of the 1950s-looking Novak and Chanel's re-issue of the classic, 2.55, all the year's favourite bags were big, leather or skin, slightly slouchy, with a mix of tough, boho and chic. Practical, and great-looking. No wonder we all wanted one!

McCartneys vs. The Fur Trade

The Not-So-Pretty Picture
According to a number of recent exposés, much of the fur clothing and accessories coming out of Eastern Europe and Asia is from dogs and cats. Why? It's cheaper than using traditional fur-farmed animals. The fur, which comes from both strays and captured pets, is often re-labelled to disguise its origins before being re-dyed and sewn. The most troubling aspect is how it all takes place: Animals may or may not be drugged before being skinned alive. Furriers say this 'preserves the fur's freshness'. And yes, a live skinning of an Alsatian – heart-wrenching noise and all – was part of the footage on recent exposés by Heather Mills-McCartney and others.

What You Can Do
Simple things like not buying fur handbags helps. So does getting involved. You can ask for a European Union ban by contacting David Byrne, European Commisioner for Health and Protection at david.byrne@cec.eu.int; and Baroness Symons, Minister for International Trade and Investment, at ministersymonsaction@fco.gov.uk. Visit www.HeatherMillsMcCartney.com for more ideas.

White, the new black

2006

After years of blacks, browns, crazy brights, metallics, prints, fur and pastels, handbag fashions take a turn towards white. Just white. Suddenly everything looks new again.

If there is one thing that can be said about the 21st century, it is luxurious. And nothing is more luxurious than a delicious high-end designer bag, even if it takes a year-long waiting list and a five figure sum to get. In the early part of the century, designer bags were coloured in rich – and expected – neutrals, including black, cordovan, brown and tan. As the years passed brights appeared in the form of shocking pink trim, red cherries, linings in unexpected shades.

DIOR GAUCHO
This roomy pouchy, saddle-like bag features Dior charms, an asymmetrical buckle, and plenty of metal detail. 'Every girl should wear one of these and go out looking for trouble', says Dior designer John Galliano.

" White is as easy as black, now that people are wearing it year-round."

COACH PRESIDENT REED KRAKOFF

Metallics had their day, as did pastels prints – especially those incorporating a designer logo (think Louis Vuitton). When it seemed there was nothing new to be had, along comes white. A colour so simple, so old-fashioned (yet so youthful), that jaded handbag aficionados fell in love all over again.

The appeal of white

In the 1990s and even early 2000s, the colour white was a no-no, especially among the hip of fashion capitals such as London, New York and Paris, and particularly for accessories. A white bag conjured images of grandma in her Sunday best, or an eight-year-old dressing-up. There was something gauche, uncool, and just plain tacky about white. Why the change? In the words of designer Michael Kors, '...we've had quite a few years of bling, bling, bling, bling, bling. To me, it's like too rich a meal. At some point, you need to cleanse your palate.' Consider yourself renewed.

WHITE AND GOLD
A princess of a bag, this boldly-shaped beauty features a dressy chain handle, plenty of room, and a lady-like look.

SCRUMPTIOUS LEATHER
With that fabulous D&G slouch, this great-looking bag boasts outer pockets... no digging through a crowded bag for mobile phones and keys. We love it!

Rent a bag

You love high end bags but simply don't have the cash (or credit) to buy a Gucci or Chanel of your own. You could opt for carrying a cheap fake, though if authenticity matters hiring your bag may be a smarter choice. Companies like Bag Borrow or Steal and Bags To Riches are popping up all over the States, Canada and UK. The gist: For a monthly fee, you can hire a designer bag. When the month is up, you return the bag with the option of choosing another. Some companies even allow you to purchase any purse you can't bear to give up. Ingenious, huh?

Index

Acknowledgments

Author's acknowledgment: I couldn't have finished *Handbags: What Every Woman Should Know*, without the support of my husband Richard Demler and our sons L.C. Pedersen and A.G. Pedersen. The women of Ladies Who Launch have generously helped with everything from contacts to photos to advice. I can't say enough flattering things about Damien Moore, Laura Watson, Jane Baldock, and the rest of the talented team at Studio Cactus. Thanks, too, to David & Charles publisher Sara Domville, and publicists Clare Owen (UK) and Greg Hatfield (US). And I must thank you, dear reader and handbag lover, for your interest. Thank you!

Studio Cactus would like to thank: Sigrid and Heinz Ivo at the Tassenmuseum Hendrikje for their invaluable contributions; Sarah Lord at Steptoes Dog for allowing us access to a vast collection of amazing vintage bags (www.steptoesantiques.co.uk); Lynn Wilson and Anna Johnson at Hêtre in Alresford, Hampshire; Jane Baldock, Alison Lubbock, Olivia Massingham, Dawn Terrey, and Laura Watson for the loan of their handbags. Also to Sharon Cluett, Sharon Rudd, Dawn Terrey and Laura Watson for design; Jane Baldock, Emily Rae and Ame Verso for their editing; Aaron Brown, Jenni Close, and Rob Walker for proofreading and research. And lastly, grateful thanks to Anna Sui, Tim Bent at Bentleys of London, Chanel, Chloé, Dior, Dolce & Gabbana, Gucci, LeSportsac, Lulu Guinness, and Philip Treacy for their wonderful images.

Picture credits

Every effort has been made to trace the copyright holders; we apologize for any unintentional omissions. We will be pleased to insert the correct acknowledgment in any subsequent edition of this publication.
Courtesy of the Advertising Archives: 111t, 120; Alamy/Homer Sykes: 88bl; Alamy/Popperfoto: 56; Anna Sui: 119br; Bentleys of London www.bentleyslondon.com: 29c; Burberry: 10br, 96crb; Capital Pictures/Alice Krige: 93tr; Chanel: 68t, 68c, 68bc, 68br, 69r, 69br, 108-109; Chloé: 122b; Christian Dior: 124clb; Dazzle: 112r; DLM Ledermuseum, Offenbach/C.Perl-Appl: 45b; Dolce & Gabbana: 125tr, 125br: 10tr; Getty Images/Evan Agostini: 99; Getty Images/Diane L. Cohen: 100bl; Getty Images/Georges De Sota: 76c; Getty Images/Tim Graham: 97r; Getty Images/Hulton Archive: 36-37, 84c, 85, 87r, 114bc; Getty Images/Roger Viollet: 70; Hêtre: 110bl, 110br, 111bl, 111br, 115bl, 115br; Jamin Puech 11br; The Kobal Collection/Paramount Pictures: 50l; The Kobal Collection/Warner Bros: 69tl; LeSportsac: 116bl, 116br, 117bc, 117br; Lulu Guinness: 9bcr, 104c, 104bl, 104bc, 104br, 105bl, 105br, 105tc, 106c, 106cr, 107br, 114br, 115tr; courtesy of Olivia Massingham: 123tl; courtesy of www.millieandgeorge.com: 114r; courtesy of the Museum at the Fashion Institute of Technology, New York photograph by Irving Solero: 48bl; Passionfruit New York: 12br; courtesy of PETA: 123br; Philip Treacy: 1c, 12tr; Photos.com: 13bl; Punch Cartoon Library: 18cra, 33cla; Rex Features/FIN: 89tc; Rex Features/MD: 94; Rex Features/ROO: 107l; Rex Features/RUS: 95br; Rex Features/SRK: 101bl; Rex Features/TB: 81tr; RKO/The Kobal Collection/Tolmie Rod: 62l; Shutterstock: Ciobanu Alexandru Cristian 114tl and 114tr, Stuart Blyth 95c, Neo Edmund 84tl, J. Helgason 86tl and 86r, Cindy Hughes 11l, JJJ 10-11 and 11-12, Eva Madrazo 9bl and 87tl, Alina Mamlyuk 9r, Alin Popescu 80bl, Aleksander Potocnik 11tr, Miguel Angel Salinas Salinas 96tl, Ljupo Smokovski 92tr, Craig Wactor 57tl; Stockybyte: 11cra; Tom Schmucker: 6-7; Tassenmuseum Hendrikje: 8c, 8bcl, 16-17, 16bl, 16cra, 17tl, 17br, 18, 18bl, 19c, 20-21, 20tl, 20b, 21, 22bc, 23, 24c, 25bl, 25br, 28crb, 29bl, 40bl, 47br, 51br, 52c, 53r, 62r, 63ca, 71crb, 76clb, 77t, 90, 102bl, 102c, 102r, 103l, 103bl, 113b; Tony Price: 25tl, 39l, 39r, 46c; Yasmena: 43bl; Zac Posen: 121. All other images © Studio Cactus

Also in this series...

Bra: A Thousand Years of Style, Support and Seduction
ISBN 0 7153-2067-X

Lacy, padded, push-up, strapless, halter, balconette, – the bra in all its glorious forms is celebrated in this sassy book for fashionable girls everywhere.

Shoes: What every Woman Should know
ISBN 0 7153 2234 6

What we wear on our feet speaks volumes about our personality and attitude to life. This sumptuously illustrated history of shoes reveals how women have been, and will forever be, shaped by their shoes.